FORGIVENESS

FORGIVENESS

A Legacy of the
West Nickel Mines Amish School

John L. Ruth

Herald Press

Scottdale, Pennsylvania
Waterloo, Ontario

Library of Congress Cataloging-in-Publication Data
Ruth, John L.
  Forgiveness : a legacy of the West Nickel Mines Amish School / John L.
Ruth.
      p. cm.
  Includes bibliographical references.
  ISBN 978-0-8361-9373-2 (pbk. : alk. paper)
  1. Forgiveness of sin. 2. Amish—Doctrines. 3. West Nickel Mines Amish
School. I. Title.
  BT795.R88 2007
  289.7'74815—dc22
                                        2007012369

Unless otherwise indicated, the Bible text is from the *New Revised
Standard Version Bible*, Copyright ©1989, by the Division of Christian
Education of the National Council of the Churches of Christ in the USA,
and is used by permission. Scripture noted KJV is from the King James
(Authorized) Version of the Holy Bible.

All photos by the author except: page 71, Jan Luyken engraving from
Martyrs Mirror; page 101, photo by Jan Gleysteen.

FORGIVENESS
Copyright © 2007 by Herald Press, Scottdale, Pa. 15683
  Published simultaneously in Canada by Herald Press,
  Waterloo, Ont. N2L 6H7. All rights reserved
Library of Congress Catalog Card Number: 2007012369
International Standard Book Number: 978-0-8361-9373-2
Printed in Canada
Book and cover design by Judith Rempel Smucker

12 11 10 09 08 07   10 9 8 7 6 5 4 3

To order or request information, please call 1-800-245-7894, or visit
www.heraldpress.com.

Contents

Author's Note

THE STORY of the West Nickel Mines School tragedy of October 2006 is one of paradoxes. A community that shuns the mass media received global press. A proverbially conservative people proved astoundingly liberal in forgiveness.

It is unspeakably hard for any community to lose its children. Although the Amish have shown an extra quotient of forgiveness, their parental tears are as salty as anyone's. Six months after the loss of two daughters, an Amish farmer could sometimes barely bring himself out to his fields. But his people hear a gracious *command*— "When you stand praying, forgive"—and a stern *warning*—"If you don't, your heavenly Father will not forgive you." This duality is at the heart of the gospel that has shaped their attitudes.

The symmetry of equally radical anger and forgiveness at Nickel Mines is so exquisite that it compels attention. After conversation with Amish neighbors, one feels an urge to share deep thoughts. Sympathetic Mennonite neighbors have asked, shouldn't more words be given to the witness of forgiveness that this episode has embodied?

Of course, publicity, sensationalism and being romanticized are negative experiences for the Amish. They don't look to journalists to broker their story, or want to see graphic book covers promising a gory tale in tourist shops. On the other hand, they do not ignore the fact that the witness which has flashed around the world is a spiritual one. They hear from Mennonite missionaries in Africa and South America that people living in violent communities have showed instant and intense interest in the theme of forgiveness.

In the present meditation, I have tried not to add a pious prurience to the anguish of the tragedy itself. Accordingly, I have very sparingly cited specific names of persons or places. Most of the brief introductory narrative can be traced to the hundreds of reports that appeared in the media, not all completely accurate, but corporately adding up to an astonishing story. The variety of sources drawn on for the subsequent reflections are indicated in the notes.

If the eleven persons shot at Nickel Mines were a soul-numbing harvest, what of the three times that many mindless killings monthly in nearby Philadelphia, or of the daily reckoning of blood in Baghdad? Children lose parents, parents lose children. In such human chaos, how do we look forward? The Amish would answer: with Christian resignation, obedience, forgiveness, mutuality and trust. They have named their replacement for the Nickel Mines schoolhouse the New Hope Amish School. We can learn from them.

Introduction

DRIVING INTO THE LUSH garden spot of Lancaster County is like entering a colorful glitch in time. As anywhere else in southeastern Pennsylvania, June is green, July golden, and October pied. But here there's also the gold of Amish straw hats, the red and blue of little girls' dresses, the color-bursts of quilts for sale, and the confessional black and gray of nineteenth-century horse-drawn buggies.

Clip-clop-clop. Radiating into twenty other states, this is no Currier and Ives dream or Williamsburg reenactment, and it is not fading. Clip-clop-clop, right past the motel window. South of the county-spanning Lincoln Highway, where there had been no Amish until the 1940s, their fat barns, multi-generation houses, and Purple Martins have redrawn the farmscape. In Bart Township, lying between Eden and Paradise, they are actually a majority.

Neat-edged fields and gardens show that this time lag isn't about poverty or cultural decay. It's about the unique thriving of an instinct that the technological sweep of the "most advanced country in the world" has not been able to dissolve. The paradox can stir incredulity, curiosity, and admiration. Also, occasionally, disdain. In 2007 a bearded pop singer's ignorant burlesque of Amish ways is all over the Internet's YouTube.

Schoolchildren on Bart Township roads—boys on kickbikes weaving by white-capped girls on Rollerblades—greet vehicles with shy waves. Tourists stealing photos of the smaller faces coo over their breathtaking innocence. These are cherished children, their community's dearest treasure, with no more thought of their families breaking up than of the North Star drifting. Such is the norm for the Plain people, whose beginnings trace back to 1525.

Among them are spiritual cousins of the Amish, the "Old Order" Mennonites, who also drive buggies. One of the latter group's bishops, a retired farmer living fifteen miles northwest of Bart, will admit he has married two thousand couples, but won't count them up in his record book. That, he demurs, would only tempt him to be "big-feelish." Not one of his couples, as far as is known, has been divorced.

The innocence of Amish childhood, as vulnerable and trusting as it gets, is only normalcy to these parents. Musing on why it so intrigues others, they recognize the obvious: "people of the world" reflect the colors of whatever happens culturally around them. They listen to popular voices, their behavior shaped by "the trend." The case is made by an Amish father in his deliberate Pennsylvania Dutch: "What happened on the other side of the world yesterday is in the newspaper today." *Wann du sie laysht, dann bisht du drin fa denke wie die annre.* "If you read it, then you're bound to be thinking like the others."

And so Amish children aren't homogenized by the mass

media. True, in their pre-baptismal teens, some of them will get a taste of cars, radios, and iPods, but nine-tenths of even those will elect to stay in the Amish family.

One should not sentimentalize the picture. While they may look saintly from some perspectives, the Amish don't see themselves as saints, and there is valid grist for critics in both print and electronic journalism. Ancient good can look very uncouth to modern observers. There are farmers who raise puppies in stacked kennels like "livestock," provoking animal rights proponents to public demonstrations. When family abuse such as appears in any society occurs among the Amish, they try to sit on it intramurally, dealing with it by bishop rather than police authority. Gendered roles are so specific that an Amish boy asks an "English" man pushing a lawnmower whether his wife is sick. No children, not even the quota of natural geniuses, are educated beyond eighth grade. In large communities, young people are often allowed, even encouraged, to get wildness out of their system in *rumshpringa* before submitting to baptism.

When they do vote in elections, the Amish vote conservative, and thus Republican. They do not publicly criticize the government even if they think it acts wrongly. They find and buy out-of-state farmland before even some of the neighbors there know it's for sale. They pay immigrant Hmong women to sew quilts they may sell from Amish porches. Some are very reluctant to vaccinate for diseases. They shy away from the media and tourists' cameras. They become exasperated with nosey academics.

As wonderfully contented as they may be when submissive, individuals who become marginal can be miserable.

There is a genre of poignant crossover tales, some by ghost-writers. The Amish are selectively anachronistic. Tourists ask why they don't see the illogic of horses pulling implements with engines on them. And why oh why do they ostracize or "shun" relatives, even close ones, who break baptismal vows?

Readers or TV viewers should consider that when the Amish faults are depicted on page or screen, it is usually, though not always, through or about persons who have had personal difficulties and are uncharacteristically ready to divulge the details. In one case a man who had joined the Amish, married an Amish wife, and then divorced her actually brought a television network crew to tape his seizing of the children she was trying to take to her home. What resulted was a "documentary" with a horse-and-buggy chase scene, close-up shots of the woman's anguished face, and helpful interjections by an unblushing, wide-eyed commentator.

While stories of unhappiness are certainly true and regrettable, and sometimes reflect systemic issues, it isn't mainly for their faults or their strangeness that the world finds the Amish interesting. If life were generally as miserable for them as some critics claim, they would have long ago faded into the macrocultural fabric. Instead, they lay down in the American landscape a marker of old-fashioned faithfulness and love, which was thrown into relief globally by their response to an unspeakable tragedy that exploded in Bart Township, Lancaster County, Pennsylvania, on October 2, 2006.

1

A Setting for Peace, Revenge, and Faith

THE HAMLETS of Nickel Mines and Georgetown cluster near the eastern end of an axis running between two Lancaster County boundaries—the Susquehanna River on the west and the Octararo Creek on the east. At each location stands a stone monument recalling a flaring of violence that transcended local importance. To the west, an upended boulder recounts the bludgeoning of the county's last twenty Conestoga natives by a vigilante gang of "Paxton Boys" in 1763. In the town of Christiana to the east, a modest obelisk names the participants in an 1851 "riot" in which an angry Maryland slave-owner was beaten to death by black women defending a fugitive husband, William Parker.

Both episodes provoked a nationwide sensation, as has the third one at Nickel Mines. While the three incidents have in common a spectacular rage and outrage, the third has added another motif: forgiveness. It seemed so stunning to many that it reverberated in the global media. But will its effect, after a brief shelf life, amount to more than another journalistic frisson?

Four miles west of Nickel Mines, in a field from an Amish farm, stands a unique clinic for "special children."

13

Its head, Harvard-trained Dr. Holmes Morton, has been honored with a MacArthur Fellowship in recognition of genius. With his wife, Carolyn, he works primarily with Amish and Mennonite neighbors who have children living with inherited physical issues. The framework of their clinic rose in a day, built barn-raising style by volunteers from among the neighbors it serves. Modestly set back from the beaten path, it is a sign of mutual appreciation between simple-living people and cutting-edge science.

In 1989 the Mortons had been thinking that there might not be a future for their intensely local project. But when the *Wall Street Journal* ran a sympathetic article, a thousand readers from all across North America sent in an unsolicited wave of contributions. Many were in the fifty-to one-hundred-dollar range, making it clear that the Amish were iconic in the American imagination. Many sympathizers don't want this unique profile of communal and spiritual values to disappear from their horizon.

The Morton facility functions at the forefront of the sophisticated genome project of the twenty-first century. Amish families have been so stable a continuum, genealogically traceable to so small a European base of DNA (some two dozen names), that as a group they provide incalculably valuable data for analysis in the field of human genetics. While feature writers journalize about problems of "inbreeding," Morton finds in his clientele scientific and relational treasure of international usefulness. For him, what the highly concentrated Amish DNA represents is a uniquely testable sample of universal humanity. In significant parallel, it is no fluke that scientists sending Voyager rockets beyond our solar system, with copper plates inscribed with suggestions of what it means to be human, included a photo of an Amish barn-raising.

In 2006 the peace of neighboring Bart Township became the foil for the chaos of a human heart overwhelmed by lust for vengeance. The grudge was not against another human being. It was against the God of a neighbor's upbringing, blamed for an infant daughter's death. The plan concocted for an ultimate blasphemy seems too hideous to be contemplated and certainly radical enough to show it was meant to leave behind an unhealable curse. Conveniently at hand were the least protected, most trusting, least imaginably deserving targets for an unthinkable sacrifice: the tender little daughters of nonresistant neighbors whose milk the revenger hauled for a living. Only partly successful, he managed to shoot ten schoolgirls, five of whom died. He had used them to show God what it felt like to grieve.

As in 1763 and 1851, the public recoiled in atavistic recognition. Revenge is one of the oldest and most recognizable human stories. While the Hebrew Bible was accruing, the Greeks Aeschylus and Sophocles were giving the motif classic literary expression. Vengeance, their dramas showed, will always both persist and fail to end vengeance. No one avenging act provides a threshold into a new revengeless era. The Athenian audience saw in life imbalances, both human and divine, that sometimes needed to be redressed by fated action. Tragic heroines like Electra, Hecuba, and Medea represented for them what is deep in human reality; their gestures, triggering unavoidable consequences, had a grandeur of scale that gave them an aura of honor. Because it is necessary, the revenge they tried to enact was seen as just, and therefore not to be limited by ordinary morality.

Viewers, emotionally wrung out by the monumental heroism visible in tragic endings, felt ennobled. They had confronted deep reality.

If testimony were needed in 2007 to show how timeless, universal, and sad this theme is, we could tune in many voices. One is enough—that of a former Liberian child soldier interviewed on National Public Radio. "Revenge is not good," is his burden. "I joined the army to avenge the death of my family and to survive. I've come to learn that if I am going to take revenge, in that process I will kill another person whose family will want revenge then revenge and revenge, and revenge will never come to an end."[1]

The Amish are Hebraic rather than Greek in mentality. At funerals, their incantatory, Scripture-weaving preaching calls easily on the book of Genesis. Unlike Christian fundamentalists, though, they do not have a flat Bible. They would not ignore a character like Lamech, who appears already in Genesis 4, gloating helplessly of a sevenfold revenge that will impress his wives. But what an Amish sermon will emphasize, especially at communion, is the forgiveness of Joseph for his murderous brethren. This is interpreted as a foreshadowing of Christ.

As for David, though a lyrical king par excellence, his character is seen as blotted by vengefulness. He is certainly not to be emulated in his fury toward the Jebusite natives of the fortress of Zion he captures, then dedicates to God. He may not build the temple that will rise there, because he is a man of blood. His boasting of hating his enemies with perfect hatred is not preached about. Nor is music-invoking Psalm 149, calling on "the faithful" to "exult in glory," sermonically useful:

Ihr Mund soll Gott erheben,
und sie sollen scharfe Schwerter in ihren Händen haben,
daß sie Rache üben unter den Heiden.

Let the high praises of God be in their throats
And two-edged swords in their hands,
To execute vengeance on the nations. . . .
To execute on them the judgment decreed.
This is glory for all his faithful ones.
Praise the Lord!

In contrast, at the very beginnings of their own history in Europe, the Anabaptist forebears of the Amish had faced, then rejected, the option of wielding God's sin-avenging sword. Choosing as central text the four Gospels of the New Testament, they emulate Jesus, not only as forensic savior, but as what Hannah Arendt called the revealer of "the role of forgiveness in the realm of human affairs."[2]

The sense of "Vengeance is mine, I shall repay, saith the Lord," quoted in both Testaments, is firmly inscribed in their inner code.

2
A Special
Atmosphere

THE AMISH PRESENCE in America is the result of harsh treatment by the governments of their original homeland of Switzerland during the period of roughly 1650 to 1730. Bernese officials then were extremely annoyed by Anabaptists (literally, rebaptizers) who refused, on the basis of faith, to attend the official church, have their babies baptized, participate in the military, and take civil oaths.

Three centuries later, when descendants of the Swiss-deriving people once expelled as riffraff appear in the media as admirably moral and prosperous Americans, many (if not all!) Swiss feel mounting shame. Even tears appear at "reconciliation" meetings, where Swiss Reformed church leaders have asked forgiveness. In 2004 some charismatic Pennsylvania neighbors deliberately challenged the Amish to make some explicit statement that would absolve the descendants of their former persecutors from the guilt of their ancestors. Somewhat bemused, the Amish wondered what this could mean, since it had always been a cardinal motif of their New Testament mentality not to hold grudges. They don't want to play verbal games.

Nor do they enjoy having their inner life depicted in

A typical Amish schoolhouse in southern Lancaster County.

tabloid journalism. A necessary element in their faith community's survival is its ability to protect its boundaries, independent of the helpful feedback constantly offered from scholars, publicists, or evangelists building the membership of independent chapels. Their manners have their own logic, not based on modern standards of "efficiency." Their "one-room" grade schools replicate the nineteenth-century rural pattern.

In their informal gatherings there is a complete lack of the paraphernalia and protocol common among their modern neighbors. No special meeting hall, no comfortable seats, no platform, no loudspeaker, no restrooms, no loud talking, no printed agenda, no minutes, no parliamentary procedure. Most significant of all is the non-self-asserting manner of conduct. There is a taboo against promoting one's own ego in any public way. The bishops sit no higher than anyone else. The meeting happens; no one "runs" it. An overt design or plan would smack of pride.

3
A Troubled Neighbor

To BE BORN AND RAISED in Lancaster County is to take its unique milieu for granted. Not just the soil's unparalleled, Amish-nourished fecundity, the buggies, and one-room schools, but also the flood of tourists clogging roads by bus, car, and RV can seem normative. The visitors have come to eat at least for a day like the Amish, shop, and be entertained. As the tourist bureau boosts, outsize family restaurants boom, family produce stands decorate the roadsides, and a Branson, Missouri-type musical facility rises. Enriched by the human flood, what began as a slide show in homes and churches has ballooned into a domed theater not far from Nickel Mines—a mini-Oberammergau,[3] where biblical narratives are spectacularly enacted with Hollywood mise en scène.

The county is full of churches, including one of the nation's largest collections of Mennonite congregations of a dozen sub-types. The Old Order Amish, the most conservative offshoot of the Swiss-deriving Mennonites, have no church buildings as such, but meet for worship, as they have met for centuries, in homes and shops. There are many other denominations and independent congregations, including Methodists, Presbyterians, Lutherans, Church of God, and Brethren. Quakerism, once a palpable presence in Bart Township, has faded.

The past half-century has seen an increasing spread of independent and "charismatic" Bible churches and chapels. Evangelical Christianity is in the majority, as is political conservatism. There's a generous component of homeschooled children. The Amish, after resisting the school consolidation following World War II, have a dozen one-room schools, with bells in traditional cupolas and outdoor privies, in every direction from West Nickel Mines. Nationwide there are well over a thousand of them.

This bucolic, Bible-drenched setting was the childhood milieu of a non-Amish man destined to suffer and inflict enormous pain. Though carrying the same name as his father, grandfather, and great-grandfather, he would prove not interested in passing it further. He was the son of a respected rural policeman who had turned to chauffeuring Amish and of a mother who homeschooled him. As the oldest brother, he fit in quietly with his siblings, attending a rural Church of God congregation with parents and grandparents. He did not stand out negatively from his neighborhood. "He seemed like a nice quiet, person," remembered a fellow church attendee.

Shy, though not antisocial, he had found teenage employment as a dishwasher in a tourist restaurant. If there was a trait people remembered, it was that he didn't look them in the eye. But there was sports with friends—shooting pool, playing card games with fellow workers, or pickup baseball and football. After work, he'd go home in his Ford pickup truck. He liked to go deer hunting with either gun or bow in northern Pennsylvania, or have a buddy to his house to shoot clay pigeons. "He was very good at it."

His friends could not recall him angry, even under stress. The best man at his wedding would say, "When I knew him, he wasn't bitter at all."

When playing miniature golf during a double date, the young man seemed so shy that he hardly talked to his good-looking, dark-haired date. They had met on a church mission trip. Though she was four years younger, the relationship held, and after a nine-month courtship Marie Welk became the bride of Charlie Roberts. They were married by her pastor in November 1996. At eighteen, she was just out of high school; he was twenty-two.

They moved into a townhouse a few miles north of Lancaster, she working as a clerk and he at hanging garage doors in the city. In a month or two she was expecting, and the young parents apparently dedicated their firstborn to the God they had worshipped since childhood. The anticipated birth, though, was a shocking disappointment. Four days after their first wedding anniversary, a little girl was born prematurely, and after breathing for a scant twenty minutes, was gone. The grieving father carried her tiny casket from church to hearse, and from hearse to grave behind her mother's Methodist church in Bart Township. Under her name on a pink, heart-shaped stone were incised the words, "Pledged to God." Whatever powerful feeling that epitaph may have carried in 1998, its words would provide a bitter commentary on what would unfold in the father's mind nine years later.

Soon after the funeral, the childless couple moved to Bart Township, not far from their daughter's resting place.

Their modular home, next to the wife's parents, was about a mile away from a typical Amish one-room, roadside school built some twenty years earlier.

Outwardly at least, the young father was all you could ask in a parent. As three children arrived, he didn't hesitate to change a diaper. Neighbors would see him kicking a ball with the kids, splitting wood, or tinkering with a Jeep he had pieced together from spare parts. He would be the one to pick up the children from the school bus. Yet there did not appear to be other persons around his house besides his family. He himself had "many good memories together" with his devout wife. But he brooded silently and steadily on the loss of the first daughter.

Anger toward the God who had allowed this pledged child to die metastasized, until by the time the other daughter was seven the father found himself aching intolerably with resentment. Telling no one of his thoughts, he let the bitterness grow to a temperature that, in his own words, he would have "never felt possible." It wasn't anything in the marriage; he thought he had "the perfect wife." But even when having "fun times" with her and the children, the thought of the loss of his firstborn would come crashing back into his consciousness, and he would "go right back to anger."

Having youthfully longed to drive an "eighteen-wheeler," he had taken a job in his wife's grandfather's milk transportation network. Picking up milk from bulk tanks in Chester and Lancaster County, many on Amish farms, he worked alone, and overnight, seven days a week. Not every family on his route found him congenial; one even made sure the children were not around when he stopped at their farm. When his heavily loaded tank truck rear-ended a Cadillac in Chester County, he emerged angrily to say it was the other driver's fault. At the deposition and arbitration hearing, he seemed to look at the woman suing him "out of the corner of his eye," but remained calm. She was awarded 7,500 dollars.

He seemed, to the Amish proprietor of a local store he frequented occasionally with the children, "a nice guy, very nice." When his children would ask for something, he "never said no." But underneath the friendly, fatherly exterior, a fearful smoldering, never shared with anyone, was approaching a kindling point. There were memories now, also unshared, haunting him with guilt over something he thought or imagined he had done as a twelve-year-old to two little girls. This scenario began to reappear in dreams, fusing its dark, erotic fascination with the mounting hatred toward the God who allowed (or even caused?) things to be.

4
From Thought to Deed

IN AN AMISH SETTING, neighbors cooperate, and little children play safely within the biblical sound of the mill and the light of the lamp. There are few surprises. Mules graze next to the fence by the roadside school. The bell rings in the cupola, and pupils murmur over their books. At twilight, the call of parents gathers them from their barnyard sport. In meeting, the preacher may chant, "The lines are fallen unto me in pleasant places. Yea, I have a goodly heritage."

Coarse stories of past evils retreat in memory like grass-healed craters. Stories of violence in American cities sound remote. True, periodic funerals mourn members crushed in their buggies by drunken drivers. Carousing adolescents are chased home by patient local police. Now and then a barn is maliciously torched. Still, it's a scene of domestic peace hardly matched in today's America.

Once or twice in a century, though, even the quietest community may have its turn with an explosion from supposedly extinct human angers. Headlines roar, and the usual bystander is quoted, "Things like that don't happen around here." Neighbors, trying to make sense of the mystery of evil, recall uneasy dreams and premonitions.

So it was in September 2006, when people working around the milk-truck driver from Georgetown thought his already taciturn manner was darkening. Then again, near the end of the month, he seemed to relax. A few miles from his home, he appeared at the Valley Hardware store to buy two packages of plastic zip ties. It was a very ordinary purchase, had it not been for other things he was systematically collecting according to a ghoulish list: three guns, hundreds of bullets, binoculars, a candle, earplugs, wrenches, nails, eye bolts. Included, for no sane reason, were two tubes of KY jelly. Even stranger, he was adding a change of clothes, toilet paper, and a bucket. Finally, there was an unexplained plank of wood with ten evenly spaced eyebolts.

Just in these days the media reported a man invading a school in Colorado, where he trapped and abused several girls before shooting himself as police closed in. While this was only the latest in a string of attacks in American schools, the story simply reinforced the contrast between public schools and those of the Amish. The Amish had no high schools, and the white, bell-crowned elementary school building in every district was the very logo of a Rockwellian landscape. The only negative was the quaintness by which they attracted the occasional car of tourists parked next to the fence.

Whatever was going through the mind of the truck driver on the last day of September, a Saturday, made no difference to his family. Neighbors saw him playing with the children. On Sunday afternoon he watched NASCAR racing on TV with a friend. Then it was time again to make the hauling route.

At one of the Amish stops lived four children who would

not expect to see their milk-hauler next morning. When he drove in their long lane, they were probably already asleep. By the time he had delivered his load and parked the shiny eighteen-wheeler, and gone home to bed himself, it was 3:00 a.m.

Monday dawned beautifully, drawing farmers into their fields for a final crop. With only four or less hours of sleep, the driver was up helping to get the older children ready for school. At quarter of nine a neighbor saw him, baby boy in his arms, waiting with other parents for the school bus to stop. When the neighbor waved, he nodded back. It was unusual for this father to see the two older children off like that, thought the neighbor, and, as they were boarding the bus, to suddenly call them back. When they came to him he knelt and hugged them both and said affectionately, "Remember, Daddy loves you."

His wife had expected him to go for a regular drug test, required for his truck-driving license. She herself headed off to the nearby Presbyterian church to lead a prayer meeting on behalf of the local schoolchildren. He borrowed a family pickup truck and went for a little more equipment at the hardware store. Now he was ready for his chosen destination, the white Amish schoolhouse a mile down the road.

As typical for Amish schools, this one was being taught by a twenty-year-old single young woman. On the wall was a motto, claiming, "Visitors brighten our days." And indeed there were visitors present that morning: a sister-in-law of the teacher and two other young women who had brought along two preschoolers. At the desks were fifteen boys and eleven girls, one of them coloring a flower. The teacher was partway through a lesson in German, and one in spelling.

At ten minutes of ten, came the sound of a pickup truck backing across the gravel in front of the porch, and the driver, in a baseball cap, came through the door with a u-shaped clevis in hand. It looked a little like a horseshoe. Standing close to the teacher, but without looking in her eyes, he asked the roomful of pupils whether they knew what this thing was and whether any of them had seen one like it lying in the road. Some of the children recognized him as their milk-truck driver, and they believed he knew some of them.

Put off by his strange manner, the teacher stopped her German and spelling lessons and calmly said that she and the children would look out for his lost item. But after he walked out to his truck, he came right back in, carrying a shotgun. He had also brought along a pistol, a rifle, a stun gun, two knives, and a bag holding six-hundred rounds of ammunition.

Frightened, the teacher slipped out the back of the schoolroom with a little girl impulsively following and ran to a neighboring farm to raise the alarm. Watching her almost flying, with feet hardly touching the ground, and clearing a fence as if it wasn't there, the farmer knew something was wrong.

Hearing her news, he immediately called 911. The dispatcher heard heavy breathing with the words, "There's a guy in the school with a gun!"

In the schoolhouse the gunman was giving orders, telling a boy to chase after the teacher. "You go get her," he warned, "or I'll start shooting!" As the boys watched in horror, he ordered the ten girls to lie down with their heads toward the blackboard, and tied their hands and legs together.

Then without explanation, he sent the boys and the adult women visitors, with their little children, out of the building. The victims he wanted, ten of them aged six to thirteen, were now helplessly in place. He carried in the rest of his equipment and began to barricade the doors with two-by-fours and a foosball table.

Back at the attacker's home, his wife had just returned from her prayer meeting. There lay a strange letter in her husband's handwriting. There was a reference to their lives, in the past tense; she had been a "perfect wife," deserving so much better a husband. "We had so many good memories together as well as the tragedy with Elise." Terrified, she immediately tried to call the cell phone that she knew he had.

At the county's emergency communications center twenty calls poured in. Then her phone rang and it was her husband, telling her not where he was, but that he would not be coming home. Rambling that he had long ago molested several girls, he stated that he was now intolerably haunted in dreams by the urge to repeat that behavior. It didn't make sense. "I am filled with so much hate," ran the shocking words on the note, "hate toward myself hate toward God and unimaginable emptiness." Reading that, she called the police and told them she was afraid he might commit suicide.

Inside the school, Roberts was asking the lined up, bound, and trembling girls to pray for him. One said, "Won't you pray for us?" At one point he gave them an order that the older girls, in Dutch, told the younger ones not to obey.

But the intruder was unrelenting, declaring, "I'm going to make you pay for my daughter."

Then, as it was clear that they were going to be shot, or worse, a thirteen-year-old from a farm he had visited the night before made an amazing request: "Shoot me first."

Within days those words would echo around the globe. Had she thought that her plea might satisfy him and that the others might have a chance to be saved? Was she playing for time? That was the interpretation of the teacher's father, who heard that the girl's full statement was, "Shoot me and leave the other ones loose." Was it simply the protective love of an oldest sister? ("Greater love has no one than this.") In any case, her younger sister followed with, "Shoot me second."

Within minutes of the 911 call from the nearby farmhouse, two state troopers, followed by eight more, arrived at the schoolhouse. Using a loudspeaker, they called out to the gunman. It only sped his operation. Dialing 911 himself, he stated that he had taken ten girls "hostage," and ordering "everybody off the property or, or else. Now!"

Threatening to start shooting within a few seconds, he hung up, and almost immediately began blasting away at the girls, hitting all ten of them in rapid succession. Hearing the shooting, police dashed for the building, as he fired one blast at them, then a final one at himself. Breaking in through the windows, they found eleven bloody bodies, five of them, including the shooter, lifeless. A sixth died in the arms of a trooper. Under the stickers of smiling faces on the bulletin board, no desk or chair was spared by the blood and broken glass, still overseen by the motto, "Visitors brighten our days."

The ensuing scene, drawing traffic from all directions, was exactly the kind that the Amish try hard to avoid. At least eight ambulances arrived, and five emergency helicopter crews were summoned. As a paramedic who had just landed in a field next to the school walked toward the building, others brought him a ten-year-old shot in the head. She was immediately flown to one hospital, then on to a bigger one in Philadelphia. As other bloody girls were also brought there, a pediatrician noticed what he had never seen before: tragedy-hardened nurses and doctors crying.

On the heels of the paramedics, the media flooded in with mobile transmitting dishes. Within hours, people all over the globe—from the BBC to Al Jazeera—were viewing the scene at Nickel Mines. The Internet lit up with conversation from China, Lithuania, Iraq, and Argentina. America had had many shootings, but this—this was the limit!

It made no sense at all, least of all to an Amish boy whose sister was shot. "I just can't see why that man thought he had to do this," he was quoted as saying. "Did he know what he was doing, or what?"

Unbelievable, said an ex-Amishman. "The innocents of the innocents!" There was no scale by which to measure such irony.

5
Whence Rage?

O N THE DAY OF THE ATTACK, the Associated Press reported a statement from the assailant's anguished wife: "The man that did this today was not the [person] I've been married to for almost ten years. My husband was loving, supportive and thoughtful—all the things you'd always want and more. He was an exceptional father. He took the kids to soccer practice and games, played ball in the backyard and took our seven-year-old daughter shopping. He never said no when I asked him to change a diaper. Our hearts are broken, our lives shattered and we grieve for the innocent lives that were lost today. Above all, please pray. Pray for the families who lost children today. Please pray for our family and children."

"It had to be some kind of anger," commented an old friend who had been called by the attacker's wife. What was most surprising to all who knew him was "that he could change like that so drastically." How could sorrow breed a resentment that could segue so grotesquely? What iron equation had locked this heart into its self-cursing logic? And how had it fused with a libidinous urge?

How, indeed, can anyone explain what motivates a

physically strong man to violate, mutilate, and kill a beautiful child? What in the name of God could be pleasurable in this? Yet the media continuously report such obscene attacks. The word *lust* is inadequate; after all it is just an old synonym for *desire* that has suffered moral slippage.

The key to understanding such behavior is that it must have a component of vengeance. "I have been wronged by life," groans a voice in the heart. "Since I'm fouled up in my own nature, I'll take vengeance on the unattainable, tormenting mirage of innocent beauty. Since I can't have it, I'll smash it." It seems possible to see in the drive for vengeance a shadowing forth of a truly fundamental problem in human nature. For this, in a Christian consciousness, the narrative of the cross becomes the key. Not Constantine's conquering cross, but the cross of the innocent martyr—the sacrificial lamb—is a guide to the nature of reality.

Nothing is ever adequate to defuse the self-cursing of a rage indulged. The soul is eaten out from the inside. As the Nickel Mines attacker wrote, what he felt was an "unimaginable emptiness." If we lack something we dearly desire, anger that someone else has it can be a motivation to prove that what they have is an illusion.

In American literature, there is no more memorable description of human rage than in the figure of Ahab, the aptly named captain of a whaling ship in Herman Melville's greatest novel. Its title, *Moby-Dick*, is the name of an enormous albino sperm whale that, as Captain Ahab had attempted to harpoon it, had ripped away one of his legs. Thus "dismasted," Ahab is permanently tortured by a lust for vengeance. Whether or not the injury he has suffered was intentional, whether or not it was fated, and whether or not there is a God behind what happens, Ahab's heart burns with a monomania for retributive satisfaction. It possesses and defines him, gradually eating out his heart, and leaving—yes, what the Nickel Mines attacker called—an "unimaginable emptiness."

Melville finally suggests that the unassuaged lust for vengeance has driven Ahab crazy, his logic making sense only within his own mind. Desperate for a target at which to strike back, he confronts the "face" of the whale. Alas, it is a broad blankness. "I think it has no feeling," Ahab rages. But that very blankness goads him more, and he tries to pierce through to the whale's heart, where "he most feels his cursed life."

"Where he . . . feels"! This is emotional language for what in our present culture is likely to have a clinical explanation. However we may describe it, it seems that the lust for ultimate satisfaction of injury, if not somehow checked, can ooze a hellish sweetness that overwhelms the fear of hell itself. But what bargain is that? To trade a moment's satisfaction for an eternity of torment is insanity. So from a standpoint like that of the Amish, one concludes that the sufferer has gone crazy. That is the kindest explanation, and the one easiest to live with. Not that it brings back the victims of the anger or makes the perpetrator's behavior less grotesque.

Is anger a necessary response to outrageous loss? The Amish, born with the same capacities as any other humans, would not think so. They are not alone in this, of course. This writer recalls being struck some twenty years ago by the simple beauty of an adolescent girl from an Old Order Mennonite family. Since the impression proved actually unforgettable, I was particularly saddened to hear some years later from her parents that she had died. Then, in a conversation after the recent Amish tragedy had occurred, the girl's mother recalled the loss of that daughter. Since the parents themselves had seen her as very "special," the loss had been doubly painful. But the notion of being "angry at God," remarked the mother, "was the last thing we would have thought of."

This was in contrast to the reaction of another family to its own loss. Devout not in the mode of their Mennonite background, but in an evangelical fellowship that boldly claimed God's special providences, they rejoiced in the healing of a family member's serious illness. The insistence of their assurance was actually a central feature of their piety, so uncharacteristic of their earlier heritage. Later, when the illness recurred and grew deadly, they again claimed this assurance. But when death ensued anyway, the proclaimed trust turned to anger—at God and at others. A target was needed for the frustration.

The key to this anger seemed to be the loss of what was considered an entitlement. When one feels one has had a deal with God—a deal that has been broken—the disappointment can fill the skies. In contrast, as will be observed below, the Amish and others like them do not feel they are in a position to announce what God must, or even will, do. They expect nothing less than mystery, and thus do not need explanations or advice from books like *When Bad Things Happen to Good People* to get their bearings.

"I don't get mad," wisecracks a motorcyclist to a friend waiting in line at a McDonald's. "I get even." This common statement is made in a tone suggesting that it's expressing a kind of emotional intelligence. To exact condign satisfaction—to inflict proportionate reciprocal injury—is considered a way of healing the injured person's frustration. People invoke something called "closure." If I must get even to have closure, and there is no object to get even with, what other outcome can there be than pain or projection onto a substitute target or madness?

What if the religions of earth's billions would encode an elemental attitude of forgiveness rather than entitlement? What if those tempted to get even would have been suffused by nursery training with the mystery of forgiveness? What if the paradigm of the cross of Christ would become the logic of the human heart, instead of providing a gilded symbol to decorate necks and crown cathedrals?

6
After the Attack

A S THE MEDEVAC HELICOPTERS roared off to hospitals, the media swarmed along the roads of Georgetown.
Amish and other neighbors gathered in clusters along fence
and ditch, in tentative postures showing their shock and
grief. It was taking authorities more than usual time to track
down some of the parents of students in the school. When
the news did come home to Amish parents, they broke down
as anyone else would have done, though without hysterics.
A mother, confirming at first sight the identity of a daughter's
body, had to be steadied as her knees buckled.

The head of the Pennsylvania State Police gave crowding
reporters a remarkably calm, candid, and respectful account
of what was known. It was almost as though something in
the comportment of the Amish was tempering the rhetoric
ordinarily expected in such briefings. Governor Ed Rendell
came and listened, then announced that state flags would fly
at half-staff. Photographers with long lenses, though kept
back by police in respect for Amish scruples, recorded all they
could. Phones began to ring nonstop at the offices of scholar
Donald Kraybill at Elizabethtown (Pennsylvania) College and
insurance administrator Herman Bontrager at New Holland.

As the confusion began to clear, reporters buzzed with a special theme. Within hours of the shooting, they heard, the grandfather of the attacker's wife had gone to the farm home of two of the girls who had been shot. As soon as he walked in, the girl's father had come to shake his hand. While Amish people are not ordinarily demonstrative, this was no ordinary moment.

When the two sat down, the grieving farmer placed his arm around the shoulder of the grieving grandfather "and said there was no grudge, only forgiveness, and that they held nothing against [the attacker's family]." This was placed in context by some neighbors, who observed that whenever Amish persons were injured or killed in traffic accidents, the Amish "always" went to the responsible persons and expressed forgiveness.

Other reports claimed that some Amish had immediately shown compassion for the stricken widow. Sent out with the evening news, that note quickly evoked viewer interest that matched the fascination for grisly facts of the attack. While Lancaster County had seemed that morning to look into "the face of hell," wrote a local journalist, "from the time the shooting stopped, we have seen God's grace in increasing bloom [in] the forgiveness and compassion the Amish have extended." In fact, it was making people around the world ponder "the meaning of life."[4]

"A strange thing happened" went a letter to the paper, referring not to the killing but the expressions of forgiveness. A Los Angeles editorialist wondered if there was anything more unimaginable than the Amish community's reaction to the tragedy: "Mourning without anger. Lack of interest in the news media—and a lack of resentment of them too. And an unwillingness, at least so far, to allow this brush with one of the modern society's worst horrors to force it into defensiveness."[5]

At New Holland, Herman Bontrager told an interviewer he was finding reporters becoming "distracted" and "introspective" as they encountered the element of forgiveness. Again and again in the media there was the note of surprise, as though forgiveness that radical was an unfamiliar concept or phenomenon. The same surprise was evident on the Internet. Relatively few bloggers were critical. There were a few responses like, "The only thing that gives me peace is knowing he will suffer for eternity," and, "His body should be dipped in pitch and hanged in chains at a crossroad." But the overwhelming tone of responders and bloggers was that of a struggle to express moral admiration.

The most eloquent and representative of the positive reactions was the commentary of Ann Taylor Fleming, a night or two after the attack, on the PBS's *NewsHour*:

> The modern media world descended en masse into this rural enclave, as if dropped back through time, poking and prodding the grief of the families and the community as a whole. And what they found and what we heard from that community was not revenge or anger, but a gentle, heart-stricken insistence on forgiveness; forgiveness, that is, of the shooter himself. The widow of the shooter was actually invited to one of the funerals, and it was said she would be welcome to stay in the community.
>
> In a world gone mad with revenge killings and sectarian violence, chunks of the globe, self-immolating with hatred, this was something to behold, this insistence on forgiveness. It was so strange, so elemental, so otherworldly.
>
> This, the Amish said, showing us the tender face of

religion at a time and in a world where we are so often see-ing the rageful face. This was Jesus' way, and they had Jesus in them, not for a day, an hour, not just in good times, but even in the very worst.

The freedom contained in Jesus' teaching of forgive-ness, wrote the German philosopher Hannah Arendt, is the freedom from vengeance, which includes both doer and sufferer in the relentless automatism of the action process, which by itself need never come to an end.

We have seldom seen this in action. So many tribes and sects in a froth of revenge, from Darfur to Baghdad. And, here in this country, so many victims and victims' families crying out in our courthouses for revenge.

To this, the Amish have offered a stunning example of the freedom that comes with forgiveness, a reminder that religion need not turn lethal or combative. I, for one, as this week ends, stand in awe of their almost unfathomable grace in grief."[6]

On the day following the attack, prayer services were called here and there in Lancaster County, drawing some 1,650 mourners to meditation, singing, and Scripture. Church bells rang in honor of the ten girls, five of whom were dead and four in hospitals. In Bart Township, the ordinarily quiet roads were busy with both Amish buggies and vans driven by non-Amish chauffeurs bringing visitors to viewings in the stricken homes. Mothers, laying out their daughters in the pristine white common in an earlier age of shrouds, encouraged the surviving siblings to touch the bodies from which souls had fled. The visitors crowding into the rooms with the old-fashioned coffins, narrow at each end, and with-out flowers, were likewise traditionally conditioned not to minimize or sentimentally disguise the evidence of death.

On Thursday, three days after the shootings, funerals were held for four of the girls (the fifth was a day later). The entire process, staggered to enable overlapping family groupings to attend more than one funeral, lasted from nine a.m. to five p.m. Fifty law enforcement personnel, backed by a plane and helicopter, blocked the access roads. Still, persistent media representatives lined a block-long section of the main road, waiting for the procession to the grave-yard. A clueless reporter, trying to get into a funeral while wearing a garish dress, tried unsuccessfully to pass herself off as Amish. As had been common in all local communities before the coming of automobiles, young fellows as "hostlers" parked horses and buggies, marked with chalk for identification, at the homes where funerals were held.

There is no singing at an Old Order Amish funeral. Two preachers, standing at the intersection of the house's two largest rooms and turning from side to side, speak with emotion but not overt dramatics. Though the Bible lies closed, perhaps on a nearby chair, the preaching, in German, links one scriptural quotation to the next. Simple analogies drive home the scriptural truths. There is no eulogy—a "worldly" concept—but earnest admonition to benefit spiritually from what has happened. The deceased girls of Nickel Mines need not be worried about; they are safe in God's keeping. In this case it was important to be reminded to forgive, and above all, to live in consciousness of the brevity of life.

Snatches of hymns can be woven into the exhortation. Especially familiar is one of the old funeral songs in the "Thin Book" used in their services. By the German pietist Ehrenfried Liebich (1713-1780), it begins familiarly, *"Nun bringen wir den Leib zur Ruh"*:

We bring the body now to rest
And with the earth let it be dressed;
Since the Creator says it must
Again be turned to earth and dust.

Here, Man, discover what you are,
Learn here what our existence is;
When sorrow, fear and need are past
Comes finally our death at last.

How swift our span of life does flee;
After death comes Eternity;
As we have spent our time while here,
Reward from God's hand will appear.

Our honor, fortune, wealth shall last—
As we ourselves—a moment past!
And thus endure both cross and grief,
As our own life, a time but brief.

Not always ash and dust we'll be,
Nor robbed of our identity,
But when our Lord appears to view,
United with our souls anew.[7]

The sight of a queue of buggies winding from the farm-yard of a funeral toward an Amish graveyard floats in memory. In Bart, mounted police just in front of the mortician's automobile, followed by the black, horse-drawn hearse, led the five processions on the main road, past the house of the attacker. His widow and children, who had been invited to the funerals, had understandably chosen not to be home.

At their plain, white-fenced cemeteries, Amish mourners closely encircle the hand-dug grave. There are no dramatic outbursts, and as soon as the ministers are through with reading a hymn and prayer, men with shovels fill the grave.

The circle does not disperse until the last of the soil is neatly heaped. This is holy drama, every step throughout the entire procedure having been ritualized in long memory. With the community itself in charge, the idea of a grief counselor or help in orchestrating the process is unthinkable. One unusual motif at the burials in Bart was the sympathetic presence of several state troopers who had responded to the shootings. This was felt by Amish observers as "really touching."

On the following day an even more impressive sight unfolded at the burial of the attacker, in the family plot behind a small Methodist church. Around the new grave, next to the pink, heart-shaped gravestone for the infant daughter whose death the deranged father had so angrily mourned, half of the circle was Amish neighbors. The widow had words of appreciation for them: "We are filled with sorrow for all of our Amish neighbors whom we have loved and continue to love. We know there are many hard days ahead for all the families who lost loved ones, and so we will continue to put our hope and trust in the God of all comfort, as we seek to rebuild our lives."

The Amish reciprocated in love. "I hope they stay around here," commented one man, "and they'll have a lot of friends and a lot of support."

Another father had told his own family, "We must not think evil of this man."

"I wish someone could have helped him out, poor soul," commented still another, who would not give the press his full name. "It's obvious that something was troubling him."

It was the kind of thing an Amish person might say. A

father who lost a seven-year-old daughter was quoted, "I never had a thought of hate in my mind."

A woman writing in to the *Budget*, reporting trouble local people had had with a young man shooting at their mailboxes and cat, concluded, "Pity the poor soul that he has nothing better to occupy his time."

Among the Amish, verbosity is negative: the more words, the more likelihood of overstatement and dilution of meaning. "I can't follow that man," says an Amish minister of a city visitor. "He talks too fast."

The Amish confession is a life and a community rather than a verbal construct. The basic attitude toward the Nickel Mines attacker had been expressed at the shooting itself by one of the Amish grandfathers, the reluctant subject of a television interview. With the camera unseen behind him, he had been asked whether he had forgiven. "In my heart, yes," was the murmured reply. And when the interviewer persisted, asking how that was possible, the answer was equally terse: "With God's help." Yet another question brought from an Amishman the explanation: "We have to forgive because Christ forgave us."

A spontaneous tide of notes and cards from every state and even foreign countries began to roll into the local post offices, bringing 5,586 letters in one day. Contributions eventually exceeding four million dollars came to the Mennonite Central Committee, Mennonite Disaster Service, Anabaptist Foundation, and the Nickel Mines School Victims Fund. Capital Blue Cross added a 500,000-dollar donation. With volunteers sorting the tubs of mail, a local business supplied food for gatherings, and five hospitals wrote off medical charges. One weekend saw the spectacle of three thousand motorcyclists rolling through the township in a demonstration of sympathy that raised a reported 40,000 dollars.

Repeated concern came from local Amish that the family of the attacker be helped with their financial needs. Reporters lingering and returning to the scene of the tragedy and its aftermath sought cautiously for persons to speak about the community. An Amishman commented, "Everybody was Amish this week. We were all in it together." Eager to have the public attention die down, but grateful for the help pouring in so incessantly, some families "could hardly get their work done." With letters to local newspapers generally praising them for their readiness to forgive, they had to accept the partly embarrassing sensation of unprecedented commendation.

After several weeks, there was an emotional gathering at the Bart Township fire hall, arranged by state police to bring together a dozen of the troopers who had first responded to the alarm with the affected families. Not all the troopers were yet over the trauma, and so a few chose not to come. Several wore civilian clothes; others were in uniform. The purpose of the meeting was to share their feelings by talking over the events of the attack. The troopers needed to know how the families were doing, and the Amish were eager to show their appreciation.

Present with their parents were three of the girls who had been shot and had been released from the hospitals. At first made quite nervous by reminders of what had happened, they became obviously at ease when they recognized several of the troopers who had come to rescue them. It was even "comforting" to them, observed one of the fathers, to converse with these unusual friends. Struggling for words, he expressed appreciation for the way the troopers had "put their hearts out on the floor," and the Amish had responded in kind.

An Amish leader, commenting on the troopers' visits to the victims' viewings, called them "our friends." There was gratitude for the police preventing the attacker from carrying out his full intention. "The way authorities stepped in to help calm the community and allow our people to . . . handle their grief as privately as possible under circumstances that made news nationwide" gave the Amish a "thankful feeling." It fit their understanding of the apostle Paul's teaching in Romans 13, that Christians are to respect the "powers that be" as ordained of God to protect law-abiding persons.

Though the Amish do not consider themselves free, as followers of Christ, to wield the kind of force necessary to control evil behavior in society, they acknowledge and even approve the necessity of governmental restraint for socially intolerable behavior. They follow such biblical directives as in 1 Peter 2:13-14: "Accept the authority of every human institution, whether of the emperor as supreme, or of governors, as sent by him to punish those who do wrong and to praise those who do right."

Tracked to its very earliest Anabaptist expression, this theme can be found addressed in the "Brotherly Agreement of Some Children of God on Seven Points," drawn up at the village of Schleitheim on the northern border of Switzerland in 1527. One of its most often remembered statements is, "The [use of] the sword is ordained by God *outside the perfection of Christ.*"

Nevertheless, governments that rule by the force of the

law, while necessary and God-ordained, are not seen by the Amish as identical to the kingdom of God. For persons who follow Christ in life, the sword is forbidden, even for self-defense. When an Amishman uses a gun, it is for peaceful purposes, such as hunting game. Otherwise he has no use for one.

Three weeks after the attack at Nickel Mines, the Amish community offered public thanks for the good work of the police, firefighters, and rescue workers, specifically "for their quick action and their protection of our privacy during the days of sorrowing and grief." Gratitude was also expressed to "the whole community, both English and Amish, for everything that was done to help carry this burden" and to "all people of all nations around the world for all the donations that have been sent to us and for all the prayers that have been offered on our behalf."

Although death could "seem so harsh," added the statement, God was comforting the community with "thoughts, dreams, and Scripture which, before, may not have been understood." In fact, there were little stories afloat, involving sightings of angels and varying memories of words uttered in the midst of the Nickel Mines attack.

Persistent expressions of sympathy came from every direction in forms of elegiac music, nostalgic painting, and solemn poetry. As the five survivors began to return from the hospitals, follow-up articles appeared in the press as late as Christmas. The Internet still echoed with comment, and the Web site Beliefnet reported that its year-end poll of the Most Inspiring People of 2006 had seen a majority vote for the Amish. Their "radical forgiveness" had "showed the world an alternative response to violence."

Expressions of amazement or at least puzzlement continued to appear. A letter to a Lancaster newspaper was headlined, "Ability to forgive is foreign to most." This was followed up in the same paper by a sampling of the views of five religious groups. A local Buddhist was quoted as saying that since for him there is no strong emotional reaction to anything, there is no motive for vengeance. There is always an attitude of openness and acceptance. In the case of the Amish girls, he observed that they must have had an affiliation with their killer in a past life that "needed to be resolved," and we should be glad that it now has been.

A Muslim imam in Lancaster County said that God forgives sins great or small, and humans are also asked to forgive. Where he differed from the Amish was in believing that while it is better to forgive, "we have a right" to take action against someone who injures us.

A rabbi stated that in order for forgiveness to be valid, the offenders must recognize that they have done wrong and are willing to change. There are varieties of forgiveness. "One cannot forgive another for what was done to third parties." Atonement for sinfulness can only be given by God.

A Presbyterian pastor cited the biblical injunction to forgive "seventy times seven, or infinitely," and told of his church's counseling center. A Catholic priest stated that forgiveness is central to both church and individual member, and that the Amish response was a reminder to all that "in the cross of Christ, violence has to stop here."[8]

A letter from an Amish reader appeared under the headline, "Why is forgiveness so foreign?" The memory of his own people was deeply marked by persecution, but from the beginning they had been taught not to harbor hate for their tormentors. Further, "we Amish do not wish to be recognized as a more forgiving church than any other denomination." Nor did it fit with the Amish outlook to call any of the girls, courageous as they may have been, "a heroine."

Another Amishman observed that the Nickel Mines tragedy had been his people's own "9/11" experience. As unprecedented as that shock had been for them was the outpouring of sympathy they were receiving from all over. Again and again they were invited to talk to reporters and even appear on national television to explain their reactions. But they simply do not live by feedback from "the public." They were not looking for a platform and quickly yearned to have the attention die down. Still, they were respectfully quoted on morning news shows, which for at least half a year could still be Googled up on computer screens.

Eight days after the attack, a most touching bit of news came from a "birthing center" in little Georgetown. One of the visitors at the school on the morning of the attack, a sister-in-law of the teacher who had been excused from the scene by the attacker, had given birth to a little girl. When asked whether she had already chosen a name, the new mother answered affirmatively with the name of one of the girls she had left behind in the schoolroom, Naomi Rose.

Before dawn on the following day, backhoes swiftly demolished the now notorious West Nickel Mines schoolhouse. Television satellite trucks parked nearby showed that members of the media had camped out all night. Though the Amish were determined to attract as little attention as possible to the process, there was a circle of other observers. Among them was a grandfather of the two girls who had told their assailant to shoot them first.

Within a few weeks the scene of tragedy was restored to pastureland.

Watching the building being razed, he confessed the sadness he felt as one who had helped to build the school and had sent his own children, who were the parents of the two girls, to attend there. But he agreed that this site was not to be an attraction for sensation-seeking tourists.

The rubble was quickly hauled to a nearby landfill, where drivers took the truckloads for dumping beyond the sight of observers. There were to be no pieces left to be hawked on eBay. In a few hours, the site of so much anguish was graded, seeded, and returned to its pre-school, pastureland appearance. It was the Amish way of moving ahead, not looking backward. Six months later a new schoolhouse would be built, this time set back in a lane instead of along the public road. Offers of donated funds and building materials exceeded what was required.

7
Approaching the Meanings

THE STORY OF THE ATTACK ITSELF, told and retold in the media, was one thing. But when it was rehearsed, the two stunning motifs—anger and forgiveness—remained inexplicable in their radical intensity. What were hearers to do with their feelings about either phenomenon? For a week or two, media pundits called on psychological and sociological experts for their insights. The focus of the present meditation will turn to themes less likely to be probed from the perspectives of the Amish themselves: their historical origins and spiritual infrastructure.

Startled by the depth of the world's sympathy, the Amish wondered what was so mysterious about their attitude. Aren't Christians to live in, not merely idealize, forgiveness? The central Anabaptist conviction is that we are not only to "believe" in Christ and receive salvation from him, but to be like him in attitude. "Let this mind be in you, which was also in Christ Jesus" (Philippians 2:5 KJV). Anabaptists have held that our relation to Christ's sacrifice is one of experiencing it as done *not only for us, but in us*. That is, for those who follow Christ, his attitude and disposition are normative, not optional or theoretic.

This seems naïve to many mainline theologians and church leaders, let alone secular people. A generation ago, famous Lutheran theologian Reinhold Niebuhr could be heard at Harvard repeating his suggestive formula: "The Mennonite [or Amish] farm is a protestant surrogate for the Catholic monastery." Another dismissive characterization of rural, Amish-type spirituality is the German word *Kühstallwärme*—the warmth (and narrowness) of the cow stable.

It will be repeatedly observed in this meditation that forgiveness, which is often difficult and counterintuitive, is for the Amish not only an initial commitment at baptism but inculcated in children before that threshold. The Plain people are puzzled when proponents of "spiritual warfare" exhort them to forgive and even suggest that, if they do not again explicitly state forgiveness for the descendants of those who persecuted their ancestors, they are guilty of not only lack of forgiveness but also of the basic sin of spiritual pride. In their thinking, their original acceptance of Christ's nature at baptism was already a nonretractable commitment to forgive.

Some persons who give up their Amish heritage in order to be more "spiritual" seem to imply that, in order to avoid pride, their Amish relatives should give up their cultural peculiarities. This is confusing when persons who make this call most explicit show less corporate evidence than before of being, in their own manner of life, an alternative to popular culture. Further mystifying the Amish is a call for "reconciliation" from persons who have themselves withdrawn from earlier fellowships of their own.

To probe these topics further might well take a reader

nto the major published studies of sympathetic sociolo-
gists John A. Hostetler Jr. and Donald Kraybill. For purposes
of meditation rather than analysis, the following pages will
continue with topics such as scriptural and historical prece-
dents, the supportive role of community, hymnody used by
the Amish, the informal logic of "shunning," thoughts from
a sister Anabaptist fellowship, and anecdotes that illustrate
basic attitudes.

8
Scriptural Paradigms

THE AMISH ARE A PEOPLE of the Sermon on the Mount, found in chapters 5–7 of the Gospel of Matthew. But while that is at the center of their outlook, they range over the whole canon, and even the Apocrypha. The names of Tobit and Sirach, unfamiliar to most present-day Protestant Bible readers, are familiarly heard in Amish preaching.

This question might be asked: Reading the same Bible as other Christians, why does the Anabaptist Amish imagination arrive at different conclusions about the use of force in human relations? Why, for example, reading the book of Genesis, would the Amish see the mild attitude of Isaac, yielding his wells to the Philistines who hadn't dug their own, as more normative for them than the God-aided, successful grasping of Isaac's son Jacob?

The answer, of course, is that the Amish view all Scripture through the prism of the Teacher who said, "You have heard it said . . . but I say to you . . ." This is the new Joseph who forgives his brothers. He is the Son of the God of Israel who loves us "like as a father pities his children." As this rabbi takes us on a journey through his people's scriptures, his own new manner of life, death, and resurrection shines on those scriptures a new light.

While this Messiah's God is the One God of Scripture, as omnipotent as ever, he calls God his Father, with the familiar word *Abba*. This is of course the same God whose merciful forgiveness was already praised in previous ages; but now a threshold has arrived. Jesus' declaration is that "the kingdom of heaven is at hand." He does not repudiate the Law so graciously revealed through Moses, but fulfills it in his person as teacher, example, and finally Lord and Savior.

Jesus calls his followers to repentance, to a "new mind." The issue of forgiveness is made definitive for them in the very prayer he offers them as a model. That is, even our asking God for mercy on our own behalf is conditioned by an acknowledgment that we will likewise forgive those who sin against us. This, Jesus emphasizes, rather than doctrinal orthodoxy, is what will identify his followers as genuine: "Not those who say, Lord, Lord, but those who do the will of my Father."

In the same Gospel of Matthew (a favorite of the Anabaptists), one of Jesus' most memorable parables makes salvation itself contingent on our own willingness to forgive. It comes in response to a disciple proposing a talmudic question, "How many times should I forgive my brother? Seven times?" The story Jesus tells is that of a man who, after being forgiven a large debt by a creditor, turns around and refuses mercy on someone who owes him only a fraction of the amount of which he himself has been forgiven. Jesus presents the wrath of the original creditor, on hearing this, as a fearsome symbol of what happens to a person who will not forgive.

It is not at all too much to say that an Amish person, taking seriously the spirit of this parable, will doubt his or her own salvation if he or she is consciously unwilling to forgive in any situation whatsoever. There is little mystery about this. What is unusual is the literalness with which the Amish accept and try to apply the scriptural teaching.

Another of Jesus' parables that is just as important for the theme of forgiveness is the one about the prodigal son. Here God is likened to a father passionately willing to forgive—even before an insulting, immature, wasteful person has repented. That readiness is what God is like. The point is driven further by the forgiving father's rebuke of an elder brother who fails to rejoice in the undeserved love given to the annoying sibling. Again, while all Christians praise this story, the Amish make it a practical test of an authentic faith. There will be no elaborate strategy to achieve this attitude. Unlike an astute pilgrim such as Henri Nouwen at the Hermitage of Leningrad, meditating for hours in front of Rembrandt's great painting of the prodigal's return, the Amish listener, sitting on a hard bench in a simple house, hearing the story chanted over and over, will absorb its message as coming straight from Christ to the human heart.

Another biblical case in point is what happens to the personality of Peter, a swashbuckling braggart whom Jesus especially loves. Peter begins as almost the opposite of an exemplar of forgiveness. Not only does he try to repudiate Jesus' intention to suffer and die in his mission of forgiveness, but when push comes to shove he is handy with a weapon. Jesus, who certainly "needs" protection then from armed Roman soldiers, crisply orders his beloved friend to disarm, since "those who take the sword will perish with the sword."

The greatest statement of all on the theme of forgiveness is in the crucifixion story itself. In the most hateful act narrated in Scripture, as human spite is doing its obscene worst, the response is one of the "victim" asking God to "forgive them, for they know not what they do." For Amish and their co-believers, this is not simply a moral phenomenon to be marveled at, but a revelation of what we are called to, via a fuller view of God. It is a view of love not as sentiment or even, in a sense, as an emotion. It is an insight into what a well-known Mennonite theologian with Amish great-grandparents called "the grain of the universe." It is the reality by which they live, hope, and die. Jesus' willingness to accept the cross confirms and illuminates all that he had taught his disciples. Forgiving love, without counting the cost, is to be their norm. It is not a devotional ideal but a command to be obeyed. It is a *new* commandment, calling for a new kind of obedience.

Beyond the four Gospels, the theme of forgiveness is at the center of the story of the first Christian martyr. The last prayer of Stephen, prayed for those stoning him to death for claiming a vision of Christ seated next to God, is "Lord, lay not this sin to their charge." Such words must have undermined the traditional conscience of young Saul, an indignant bystander watching with approval as Stephen's perceived insult to Saul's religion was being avenged.

After he had become a Christian apostle with a changed name, the formerly vengeful Paul would enjoin on Christians the same outrageously forgiving attitude he had observed in Stephen. To accept it, they would obviously have to be "not conformed" to this world's attitudes toward revenge. Rather, Paul asks them to

bless those who persecute you; bless, and do not curse
them. . . . Do not repay anyone evil for evil. . . . If it is possible, so far as it depends on you, live peaceably with all.
Beloved, never avenge yourselves, but leave room for the
wrath of God; for it is written, "Vengeance is mine, I will
repay, says the Lord." No, "if your enemies are hungry,
feed them; if they are thirsty, give them something to drink;
for by doing this you will heap burning coals on their
heads." Do not be overcome by evil, but overcome evil
with good. (Romans 12:14, 17-21)

Those remarkable words were addressed by the former
persecutor of Christians to threatened Christians living in
Rome. To others in Colossae, Paul was just as direct:
"Clothe yourselves with compassion, kindness, humility,
meekness, and patience. . . . If anyone has a complaint
against another, forgive each other; just as the Lord has forgiven you, so you also must forgive" (Colossians 3:12-13).

Even rough and ready Peter, tamed by his faith in the resurrected Lord he had once betrayed, would be credited with
the same unmistakable convictions: "Have unity of spirit,
sympathy, love for one another, a tender heart, and a humble mind. Do not repay evil for evil or abuse for abuse; but,
on the contrary, repay with a blessing" (1 Peter 3:8-9). This
is not conventional self-protecting religion.

How much plainer, the Amish must wonder, could the
New Testament Scripture be? What is the mystery here?
What's really strange is why Christians in general do not
hold each other accountable for the behavior so plainly
described. What is hard to explain is why Christians, seeing
forgiveness extended, can call it "foreign."

9
Anabaptist Precedents

SCHOLAR JOHN A. HOSTETLER, who was born into an Amish home, observed that for his people the past is alive in the present. They constitute a wing of the Anabaptist movement that emerged in Switzerland and south Germany in the stormy reform mood of the mid-1520s. It was led by persons questioning the integrity of their church, whose encrusted authority was intertwined with and enforced by civil government. Awakened by the ideas of Martin Luther and Ulrich Zwingli, and after restudying the Scriptures in unofficial cell-gatherings, they imagined that they should begin over. As a young leader named Conrad Grebel of Zurich put it, they should "work with the Word [scripture] to form a church of Christ."

Of course there already was a church, to which everybody belonged. But the passionate critics of Zurich felt that a society in which every infant was baptized did not reflect what they read about repentance in the newly available words of Christ. When they then began to baptize repenting adults—all of whom had been christened as infants—they were immediately called "rebaptizers," an ancient name for a heresy punishable by death.

Alarmed Catholic authorities did indeed call Anabaptists heretics, while Lutheran and Reformed regimes saw them as guilty of civil disobedience. Both kinds of authorities levied the death penalty, the former by fire and the latter by beheading and drowning. Torture was common in either case.

For the next three centuries, intermittent confiscation of property, imprisonment, and expulsion were the lot of Anabaptists in Switzerland. The "Brothers" grew accustomed to being mistreated and to their status of noncitizens. When persecution grew particularly harsh in Zurich from 1635 to 1645, they drew up an anguished accounting of farms confiscated and children removed from homes.

Even in complaint, however, they tried to make it clear that they were not looking for retribution on those treating them unfairly. "No one should take the idea from us," stated one writer, "that we write this up out of vengeance and bitterness, but only so that our possessions and tribulation will not be forgotten, and especially by those who come after us."[9] The centuries-long experience has indelibly imprinted Amish memory and identity. The resultant attitude is one that claims no rights, while rejoicing in being tolerated in a society that disagrees with some of its most central tenets.

At the time of the American Revolution, the Amish joined Mennonites and Dunkers in a statement that they wished to be "helpful to all and hurtful to none." In Bart Township, this attitude has led many of their young men to serve in the local fire company. A familiar sight after a natural disaster is a volunteer crew of Amish men and women, every one in motion. Mennonites returning from cleanup work in Mississippi after the Katrina hurricane brought back reports from victims of the flooding that the first persons to arrive on the scene had been Amish. In one case, they observed, it had been the pacifist Amish who had cut a path with their chainsaws to get National Guard personnel to the scene of destruction.

The Anabaptists, who called each other "brothers and sisters," originally dreamed of being like the first Christians. They looked at the Sermon on the Mount as a guide for ordinary living. Such biblical literalism was viewed by Martin Luther, to whom Conrad Grebel wrote an inquiring letter, to be a kind of fanaticism. Whereas Luther valued the radical statements of the Sermon as describing what Christians *ought* to aim for, he thought it only realistic to admit that they never *could* live up to it. Or at least, only specially dedicated persons, in disciplined small groups, were likely to try. In comparison, the Anabaptists were ready to declare the Sermon definitive—even when it called for loving one's enemy or refusing to swear an oath. In brief, they insisted on radically ethical living. Of course the world was not likely to understand. But wasn't that the lot of Jesus himself?

Anabaptists in Switzerland soon found that the macro culture, though Christian in name, would not accept a Christianity that cost the risk of following Christ to death. In fact, the official Reformed church of Zurich was now encouraging a government that executed one of Grebel's closest friends for baptizing, expelled another (who was later burned to death by Catholic authorities), and would have quickly executed Grebel himself had they caught him before he died of natural causes.

Under these conditions, the young fellowship concluded that only those who were willing to take up the cross, hazarding the loss of possessions, family, and life itself, were the kind of disciples Christ called for. They were disappointed to see that what they considered to be a true church is likely to be a minority in an environment that is hostile, even while calling itself Christian. The true church, they decided, is held together not by governmental force, but by noncoerced love.

These conclusions were not reached overnight nor without some negative, even bizarre, experiments in a variety of settings, which taught painful lessons. Most damaging, before the Swiss Anabaptists had settled into quiet rural enclaves, was a violent episode in a north German city that gave the name Anabaptist a sinister ring. It was triggered by prophecy-fascinated persons who were convinced that God was about to take literal vengeance on corrupt humanity. In fact, it was their bloody Anabaptist takeover of the city of Münster in 1534 that alarmed a nonviolent leader into stepping forward to dissociate his people from fanaticism. This was the former priest Menno Simons, of the Netherlands, who gathered into a covenanted fellowship a circle of Anabaptists who confessed nonviolence as the definitive teaching and example of Christ.

Menno's role as standard-bearer was confirmed by his prolific pen. Like the Swiss Anabaptists, he was a radical, and like them, a nonviolent one. He had seen too much spiritual craziness to approve of enthusiasm as its own guide. On the title page of every one of his many publications was a statement from the apostle Paul: "For no one can lay any foundation other than the one that has been laid; that foundation is Jesus Christ" (1 Corinthians 3:11).

It is significant that in line with this concern, both northern and southern European Anabaptists, though ethnically unrelated, firmly welded together *radical* obedience to Christ and *conservative* moral behavior. Appreciating this duality is essential to understanding Amish attitudes.

Though the various groups who had used force tended to fade rapidly out of existence, the negative impression they had left worried authorities wherever any kind of Anabaptism, however quiet and peaceful, appeared. As for Menno, his name would be gradually taken up by the peaceful Anabaptists both north and south in Europe, and among their spiritual offspring in many countries and languages.

For the first century and a half in America, the Mennonite/Amish version of the Anabaptist tradition was totally identified with the Christian "nonresistance" of the "Swiss Brothers." This had been toughened into their heritage through three centuries of their life on small farms in remote enclaves in the foothills of the Alps. Whereas among the most "progressive" American Mennonites a softening of this absolute commitment began to occur in the mid-nineteenth century, it has remained definitive for all carrying the Amish name and for all Old Order Mennonites.

They do not subscribe to the idea that since Christ was divine, the standards by which he lived are too high for his disciples to require of each other. They believe it is normative for Christ's followers to suffer for the sake of his truth. Though they rejoice in having found a country to live in whose government treats them graciously, 480 years after the Schleitheim Confession they have not left its outlook of two opposing "kingdoms"—those of Christ and "this world." And they mean to stick with it at any cost, believing that their salvation is intertwined with it.

The Amish are a wing of the Swiss Anabaptists that became a covenanted fellowship under the leadership of a tailor and bishop Jakob Amman, of the Canton of Bern. Coming from the Simmental in the "Oberland" south of Thun, an area notably more conservative than the already famously conservative canton as a whole, Amman became the point man for Swiss Brethren preferring a strict application of church discipline. His "Amish" following took form in 1693 and 1694, before most of the Swiss Brethren had accepted the northern name of Mennonite. Thus, though technically the Amish never were "Mennonite," they share the identical pre-1693 Swiss and Alsatian background of their Mennonite spiritual cousins. Even the confession of faith to which they subscribe was written by a Mennonite pastor in Dordrecht, Holland, in 1632, and confirmed in 1660 by Swiss Anabaptists who had moved to Alsace.

Probably the most impressive icon of Mennonite memory is Dutch: a monumental volume of persecution stories entitled *Martyrs Mirror*. First published in 1632 by a minister also from Dordrecht, it includes a compendium of accounts of gruesome trials brought on Anabaptists by European governments both Catholic and Protestant. It is still vigorously kept in print by America's Plain people, to remind their oncoming generations of what it cost to establish and keep their cross-bearing identity. As a saga of faith surviving fire, sword and water, it was considered so important to the first Mennonites of Pennsylvania that they had it translated into German and published in Lancaster County before there were even bridges across the streams.

The Jan Luyken engraving of the Dirk Willems story in the 1685 edition of the *Martyrs Mirror*.

The incredible project was actually the largest volume to be published in North America before the Revolution.

Though this *Mirror* had originally appeared several decades before there was a separate Amish fellowship, the history it enshrines is claimed as much by them as by any other Anabaptist-deriving group.

The author's commentary adds to horrified protest the recognition that the way of Christ is one of revengeless forgiveness. Perhaps its most often-told story in recent years is of Dirk Willems, a Dutch Anabaptist who tried to escape a pursuing constable by running across a frozen canal. When the official broke through the ice and was in danger of drowning, Willems knew that the only Christlike thing was to help his enemy. So he returned and saved his pursuer.

Then, the story heart-rendingly proceeds, the constable is persuaded by accusing bystanders to arrest Willems, who is sentenced to burn at the stake. The ensuing death scene is horrible almost beyond telling—far more painful than those at Nickel Mines. The story's impact is so starkly ironic that few who have read or heard it forget it. There are Mennonites who confess that it has left a lasting imprint on their spirit. In some editions there is even an etching by one of the Netherlands' finest artists to illustrate the story. Even the modern liberal Mennonites cherish and reproduce the visual image of the unforgettable rescue.

The need of yielding one's self sacrificially is woven deep in the Anabaptist psyche. "If the Anabaptist stories are about anything," writes a Mennonite professor of rhetoric, "they are about weakness triumphing over strength, about unlikely and imperfect communities of faith becoming agents of witness to God's inbreaking peaceable reign."[10]

There is what might be called a tragic sense, a recognition that there are tears in the nature of things, implied in the worldview the Amish transmit to their children. The baptism to which they are called is threefold: not only of Spirit and water, but also of blood. That is, sharing the suffering of Christ is the model of self-giving. Certainly, for anyone steeped in the atmosphere of the great *Mirror*, there will be an uncanny recognition of the impulsive response of the thirteen-year-old girl at Nickel Mines who, when she understood what was about to happen, said, "Shoot me first." Such a reflex, which a secular society may wish to call heroism, was simply a yielding to the commandment to love that she had learned in what is recently being called "spiritual formation." And the second sister, who added, "Shoot me second," and has survived her wounds, becomes a living character in the extended story of the ancient tome, the presence of which still broods in thousands of Plain homes.

Another historical point may enrich the understanding of Amish spirituality. Relatively few people in the eastern United States realize that the Amish have more Anabaptist cousins than Mennonites. A third grouping called Hutterites thrives today in states west and northwest of the Missouri River and in western Canada. Their origins coincide with those of the Swiss Anabaptists, and they have preserved the same radical sense of submission to Christ. What has distinguished them from other Anabaptists is their choice, made in the very first years, to practice "community of goods." As a result, from three centuries before Karl Marx and into the twenty-first century they have practiced a Christian communism.

Like the Amish, the Hutterites dress simply, reject all oaths, decline military service, and strenuously preserve centuries-old patterns of life and worship. Living in hundreds of colonies from South Dakota to Alberta, they are bilingual, speaking a German dialect from Austria (as the Amish keep their "Pennsylvania Dutch" based on Swiss-Palatine German). Like the Amish, the Hutterites are growing numerically, though not without inner stresses. And, as with the Amish, their church life is ordered in a way that calls every member to account by the plain standards of the Sermon on the Mount. With them, the concept of membership is like that of the Amish, one of whose bishops put it crisply: "There is no happy medium. You are either in or out." "Full surrender of the individual" is the necessary Hutterite keynote.

Also like the Amish, the Hutterites have a historic memory of suffering. The sorrowful news from Nickel Mines in Pennsylvania elicited from them a brotherly sympathy, in words that confirm their sharing of a recognizable spirituality. Whereas the Amish might cite the writings of Menno Simons or the *Martyrs Mirror*, a Hutterite from Alberta called up thoughts from his own people's classic author, Peter Riedemann. His *Accounting of our Religion, Teaching and Belief*, written in a Hessian prison, was printed in 1565. From this vision the Albertan drew a description of the character of the fellowship of Christ. It was to be a "church of grace and love, where vengeance dare not abide, and where nonresistant love, always, needs to fill the void and emptiness of human existence, transforming it into the meaningful life in the Spirit, as lived out by our Lord, the Christ, himself."

Whereas Amish and Hutterites—and Anabaptists in general—tend to be described by unfriendly critics as trying to earn their salvation by their discipline and "good works," their own confessions of what is at the heart of their faith point otherwise. It is not that they trust their works, but that they cannot see the presence of faith unless it is shown in behavior. Riedemann's *Accounting* certainly places the source of faith not in human effort, but prior to human response: "If the Word is heard and believed, then faith is sealed with the power of God, with his Holy Spirit. . . . That person has been made into a new creature, a new person after God's likeness, and has become renewed in this likeness. Whoever is born in this way should receive baptism as a bath of rebirth." Again, it is God's Spirit, not human effort, that "leads people into all truth, motivating all they do and fulfilling God's will. In that way people begin a new life in the power of God. . . . 'Whoever is in Christ, is a new creature.'" [11]

These are words that would be owned by any thoughtful Amish person. They help us to see how the act of Christian forgiveness is not a strategy or skill, but the fruit of a radical reorientation after which we no longer count jealously to seven. With Christ we breathe the free air of seventy times seven.

10
Singing Forgiveness

AMISH SINGING takes its participants out of their century into another era, with an antique, Swiss-sounding version of the German language and a different sense of time. People hearing it for the first time are baffled and bemused, usually wondering how anyone gets meaning out of the long-outdated, interminable, weaving melodies, sung vigorously in unison. Unlike scholarly monks and nuns who may have an analytical, linguistic enjoyment of preserving timeless Latin phrasing, the Amish are simply keeping what they have always had. For them in such things, the concept of obsoleteness has little relevance. Repetition, patience, and familiarity are the welcome modes of reverence. Every Sunday the second song is the same.

But make no mistake, for those willing to take it seriously, there is spiritual energy living under this traditional surface, in texts that are revealing and powerful, and that are gradually embedded in conscientious singers. Because these texts might be the last place observers would look for insight into Amish faith, it will be worth our while to hear from several.

On their closely set, backless benches in home, shop, or

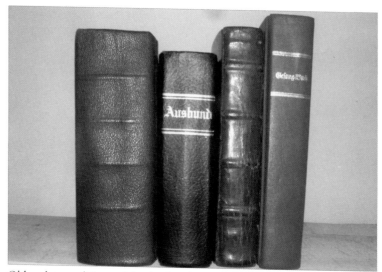

Old and new editions of the *Ausbund* ("Thick Book") and *Unpartheyisches Gesang-Buch* ("Thin Book") used by the Amish in singing.

barn, the Amish sing from two books, a "thick" one and a "thin" one. The thick one, with texts but no musical notes, is the earlier, with songs dating as far back as the 1530s, only a decade or two after the Anabaptist beginnings. Entitled the *Ausbund* (Selection), it was first placed in print in 1564 with the title *Some [fifty-two] beautiful Christian Songs as they were written and sung through God's Grace in the Prison at Passau by the Swiss Brothers.*

The jailing of these singers had happened in 1535, less than two months after the violent episode at Münster had frightened Europe's rulers. It was in that suspicious atmosphere that a totally peaceful cluster of Anabaptists, trying to travel home from Moravia to Germany, had been arrested. Before long their number totaled about sixty. Their desolate lodging was the dungeon of the powerful Oberhaus Castle overlooking the junction of the Inn and Danube Rivers in present-day eastern Bavaria.

Few Amish singers, of course, can trace this story to its beginnings (though an Amish writer from within a few miles of Nickel Mines has recently published a book on the subject). But words written and sung back then—whether in exhortation, complaint, or joyful celebration—still flow with feeling from Amish lips across North America. Nearly seventy of the *Ausbund*'s songs remain in continuous use. Each antique syllable is sung slowly enough to be savored.

The prisoners at Passau composed in the Meistersinger tradition of humble workmen singing at their trades. We may wonder if they had a copy of the Scriptures to work with, or whether they had to depend on memory. Their prosody is of course quite ordinary, mere doggerel by literary standards. When read in prose English translation, it tends to lose most of its emotional effect. Keeping at least a metrical equivalent helps to suggest the original earnestness.

Most prolific of the group arrested at Passau was Hans Betz, a weaver and "evangelical preacher" from Bohemia (present-day Czech Republic). He died after a few years of imprisonment, but not before contributing twenty-four songs. One of these, based on the Sermon on the Mount, is still regularly sung by the Amish. Nicknamed the *Berglied* (song on the mountain), it is used on the Sunday when the preachers take the Sermon on the Mount for the text. In the third stanza we hear Betz carefully setting up a marker. He has a specific point to make about attitude:

> *Die Wort thut Christus sprechen*
>> The word we hear Christ speaking
> *Daß man gelassen wird,*
>> Is: one should be resigned,
> *Sein Selbstwillen thu brechen,*
>> His selfishness be broken
> *Allhie auf dieser Erd.*
>> Right here upon this earth.
> *Alsdann wirst du umfangen*
>> Then you will be encompassed
> *Mit wahrer G'lassenheit,*
>> With true *Gelassenheit*,
> *Des Geists Armuth erlangen*
>> In poverty of spirit
> *Die würkt Reu und das Leid.*[12]
>> That works rue and regret.

The key word here, *Gelassenheit*, means "yieldedness" or "submissiveness" of spirit. It is the repentant acceptance of the sacrificial spirit of Christ that reverses what is usually considered "normal." The new norm is sacrifice of myself and loving mercy for others.

Of course people living in a modern democratic society meet such an attitude with great suspicion. It is even considered a rejection of the responsibility to face life positively. But in any case, without understanding its centrality to the Amish mentality, one will make only superficial sense of why a people in the world's richest country chooses so humble a manner of life and demeanor. Only a recognition of this profound acceptance of Christ's own example of yieldedness will place the phenomenon of Christian forgiveness as practiced by the Amish in its proper light.

Writing out of cruel imprisonment, the early Anabaptist singers were not feeling theoretical, and their prayers for help to forgive were anything but rote. It may not have been easy, but they felt it right and necessary to echo the Lord's Prayer:

> *Herr Gott Vater, wir bitten dich*
>> Lord God, Father, we pray to you
> *Für all die uns beleiden,*
>> For all who bring us suff'ring,
> *Du wollest ihnen gnädiglich*
>> That you will, in your graciousness,
> *All ihre Sünd verzeihen.*
>> Grant all their sin forgiveness.
> *Dann sie doch nicht erkennen thun,*
>> Because they do not realize
> *Was sie an uns gehandelt hon,*
>> What they have done to us so sore;
> *Wollst ihn'n dein Gnad verleihen.*[13]
>> May you grant them your mercy.

The *centrality* of forgiveness is unmistakable.

As time went on, songs from other Anabaptist writers were added to the *Ausbund*, which, for fear of church and state authorities, had to be printed and circulated without a publisher's name or location. Among the better writers was a shoemaker named Hans Büchel, born near Salzburg around 1520. One of the five songs by him in the *Ausbund*, number 71, is actually an acrostic based on his name. Especially impressive is a song he wrote after attending a debate between Anabaptists and Lutherans near Worms in the Palatinate in 1557. Not yet forty then, he was profoundly shocked and discouraged when, after the discussion, the government announced the death penalty for Anabaptists. Wondering if there had ever been a worse time for Christians, Büchel began a twenty-stanza song:

Ein g'fahre Zeit vor nie erhört
> A time of peril never heard

Seit Gott erschuf Himel und Erd,
> Since God created heav'n and earth,

Ist's nie so übel g'standen,
> Things never stood so evil,

Als jetzt bezeuget Sonn und Mond,
> As witnessed now by sun and moon,

Die Stern so an den Himmel stond,
> And stars that in the heavens stand,

In Deutsch und Welschen Landen.
> In German and lands foreign.

All Ehrbarkeit hat sich verkehrt,
> All honesty has been reversed,

Die König, Fürsten, Herren,
> Kings, lords, and other rulers

Regieren jetzt das Geistlich Schwerdt,
> Now rule with the spiritual sword,

Falsch Propheten sie lehren,
> While untrue prophets teach them.

Der Fromm weiß schier nimer wo nauß,
> Good people don't know where to go;

Man findt oftmals vier Glauben
> One oft finds four persuasions

Jetzund in einem Hauß.[14]
> Now in a single house.

As confusing and dangerous as life had become, the Anabaptists taught that they could not give in to a natural impulse of revenge. Rather, the spirit of Christ should rule their attitudes. Thus, in stanza 11 Büchel exhorts his friends to obey the Sermon on the Mount:

Geistliche Frucht, Lieb sanften Muth'
> Spiritual fruit, soft-hearted love

Thu jederman beweisen.
> To everyone be showing.

Den Feind, der dich betrüben thut,
Your enemy, who seeks your hurt—
Sollt du sanftmüthig speisen,
You shall in kindness feed him.
Barmhertzigkeit, o Bruder mein,
Mercifulness, O brother mine,
Thu jedermann erzeigen,
To all be demonstrating
Gleich wie der Vater dein.
Just as your Father does.

Wie du in Vater Unser hörst,
As in the Lord's Prayer you hear,
Vergib die Schuld wie du begehrst,
Forgive the debt as you'd desire,
Trag brüderlich Mitleiden.
In brotherly compassion.
Erspiegel dich im Herren Christ,
Show in yourself our Lord and Christ,
Leb auch also ohn arge List
And live without angry desire,
Nachred solt du vermeiden.
Slander you must be shunning.
Halt dich pur, lauter, keusch und rein,
Keep yourself pure, sweet, chaste, and clean,
Thu all's zum besten kehren.
Turn all things for the better.
Vermeid auch allen bösen Schein.
Avoid all bad appearances.
Die Freundlichkeit des Herren
The Lord's nature of friendship,
Laß kund werden vor jedermann.
Make evident to everyone:
Was du von mir wilt haben,
"What you'd from me be having,
Solt auch ein'm andern thun.[15]
Should be to others done."

Stanza 14 returns to this theme, driving the thought even further:

> *Dein Feind lieb auch, aus Herzens Grund:*
>> Love your foe too, within your heart—
> *Die dich vermaladeyen,*
>> The one who vilifies you;
> *Den'n red du wohl zu aller Stund,*
>> Speak kindly to him at all times,
> *Solt ihm auch rathen, leihen.*
>> Give loan and counsel to him.
> *Das ist der Grund und Fundament,*
>> Such is the base and principle
> *Dabey ein Freund des Herren*
>> By which a friend of Heaven
> *Hie soll werden erkennt.*[16]
>> Shall here be recognized.

How might it feel to sing slowly across such simple, radical but unmistakable teaching? The peacefulness it presents is based on nothing less than the character of the God being worshipped. Certainly any person or group absorbing such words will not have a conventional attitude toward enemies. Deliberately savoring every thought of the stanzas, returned to every year when the preacher's text is the Sermon on the Mount, will color a worshipper's mind.

Of course, for Amish singers, the obsolete Swiss-German diction, with its deeper flavor than the Pennsylvania Dutch of daily life, may add a mystical effect. But the experience is not only antique; it is just as much in the moment as in the immemorial echoes it awakens. And as radical as the words may seem, when they are repeatedly called up and shared, they come to make more sense than other options. They fit nto a divine logic in which "the foolishness of God is wiser than men; and the weakness of God is stronger than men" 1 Corinthians 1:25).

When life throws up a tragedy, a singer whose heart is shaped by such logic does not have to go through a process of deciding to forgive. The decision has been made at baptism, "on bended knee," into the school of Christ.

The *Ausbund* has been called the oldest Protestant hymnal in continuous use. And even most Amish, who refer to it as their *Dick Buch* (Thick Book) eventually felt the need of more breadth than contained in its martyr ballads and sermonic stanzas. Such a variety had become available when Lancaster County Mennonites updated their singing in 1804. Their *Unpartheyisches Gesang-Buch* (nondenominational songbook) published that year, borrowing many Lutheran chorales and Reformed hymns, also kept sixty-eight of the less polished songs in the *Ausbund*. Eventually taken up by the Amish as their *Din Buch* (Thin Book), the Mennonite *Gesang-Buch* has had an astonishingly long run of editions and is in fact reprinted every few years. Much of the demand is from Amish communities spread across the country.

One of the *Ausbund* songs that the Lancaster Mennonites transferred to their *Gesang-Buch* was another gift from the Dutch Mennonites. Placed by the Lancaster Mennonites as number 1 in their book, it has been given an iconic place in Amish worship. This is the *Lobsang* or *Loblied* (Song of Praise), written by Leenaerdt Clock, that is sung second every Sunday in Amish congregations all across America, "*O Gott Vater wir Loben Dich.*"

O God, Father, we worship you,
And celebrate your goodness,
That you, O Lord, so graciously
Anew have shown unto us,
And led us, Lord, together here,
To be admonished by your Word.
Give us grace to receive it.

Open your servants' mouths, O Lord,
And thereto give them wisdom,
That they may rightly speak your Word
That leads to righteous living,
And fitting is to give you praise—
Give us the hunger for such food;
This is our hearts' desire.

Give understanding to our hearts,
Light for our earthly journey,
That your Word might be known in us,
Leading to pious living
And living in true righteousness—
Always attentive to your Word,
Thus undeceived remaining.[17]

These familiar words, to a slow, hardly recognizable version of the sixteenth-century chorale tune "*Nun Freut Euch Lieben Christen*," are the unforgettable heritage of anyone growing up Old Order Amish. A Mennonite man in his fifties, recalling it from his childhood, confesses that he can never hear it sung without weeping. Sometimes the voices are ungainly and harsh, but there are also voices of great character, some with a natural, irrepressible vibrato. After a wedding meal, a blend of singing and socializing may persist until twilight falls. (While the singing in the Sunday worship is always of the traditional type, young people are not denied

heir own preferences for Sunday evening social singings.
There the music may range from sedate to raucous until the
ound is little different from that of an old-fashioned hoe-
lown, complete with amplified guitars.)

On a Saturday several months after the Nickel Mines
ragedy, some Amish and Old Order Mennonites gathered
n Lancaster County for an informal singing from the *Din
Buch* used by both groups. At one point a particular selec-
ion, number 235, was pointed out as especially appropri-
ite to what had recently happened. Not based on Scripture
passages, it is one of the very few songs in the *Gesang-Buch*
for which no author is known. Since most of the other
ongs are by well-known Lutheran and Reformed poets, it
seems likely that this one is from Anabaptist authorship. Its
presence suggests that the editors of 1804 may have made
a special effort to include the theme of nonresistant love, a
teaching the Mennonites could hardly acquire in full
Anabaptist expression from other sources. It certainly
would be hard to find a clearer explanation of the reason
for forgiveness than in such a song.

> *Liebe nicht allein die freunde,*
>> Do not love only those friendly
> *Wo ihr Christien heißen wollt:*
>> If you'd be a Christian called;
> *Liebet auch die ärgsten feinde,*
>> Love also your worst opponents
> *So wird euch der himmel hold.*
>> If you'd be for heaven bound.
> *Wer den zorn kann überwinden,*
>> He who overcomes his anger
> *Der wird bey Gott gnade finden.*
>> Will the grace of God discover.

Alle gaben, alle schätze,
> Every gift and every treasure
Die dein herz dem Höchsten bringt,
> Your heart to the Highest brings,
Laufen wider das gesetze,
> Is but law-defying gesture
Wo man nicht den zorn bezwingt;
> If one's anger's not o'ercome.
Opfer-gluth und eiferflammen
> Sacrifice and flames of anger
Stimmen nimmermehr zusammen.
> Never can be in agreement

Liebe treulich, die dich hassen;
> Love sincerely those who hate you,
Segne diesen, der dir flucht;
> Blessing those who curse at you;
Trachte den nicht zu verlassen,
> Don't maneuver to forsake the
Der dich zu verderben sucht;
> One who seeks to injure you.
Wohl thun ist bey dieser sache,
> Doing good, in such a matter,
Glaub es mir, die beste rache.
> Believe me, is the finest vengeance.

Wer die liebe weiß zu hegen,
> He who knows how to be loving,
Giebt sich keinem feinde blos,
> Takes no one as enemy,
Und des himmels gnadenregen
> And the rains of heaven's mercy
Fällt ihm richtig in den schoos;
> Rightly to his bosom falls.
Wer hergegen feindschaft übet,
> Who in contrast works contention,
Wird nur durch sich selbst betrübet.
> Will his own self be tormented.

Höchster! Dessen wunder-güte!
>   Highest! whose amazing goodness
Uns das lieben anbefiehlt;
>   That same love on us enjoins;
Lenke, bitt ich, mein gemüthe,
>   Guide, I pray, my inner feeling
Wann der Satan auf mich ziehlt,
>   When the Devil aims at me,
Und auf seinen sündenwegen,
>   And, along his pathways sinful,
Mich zur feindschaft will bewegen.[18]
>   Me to enmity would kindle.

Amazingly, the song following the one above, with a likewise unknown author, is on the very same Anabaptist-stressed theme.

Nie will ich dem zu schaden suchen,
>   Ne'er will I seek the one to injure
Der mir zu schaden sucht.
>   Who seeks to injure me.
Nie will ich meinem feinde fluchen,
>   Ne'er at my foe will I throw curses,
Wenn er aus haß mir flucht.
>   If he from hate curse me.

Mit güte will ich ihm begegnen,
>   With good I will seek to approach him
Nicht drohen wenn er dorht.
>   Nor threaten, if he does;
Wenn er mich schilt, will ich ihn segnen;
>   If he blames me, I'll speak him blessing,
Dies ist des herrn gebot.
>   This is the Lord's command.

Er, der von keiner sünde wußte,
> He who was innocent of sinning,

Vergalt die schmach mit huld,
> Forgave insult with grace,

Und litt, so viel er leiden mußte,
> And bore all that he had to suffer,

Mit sanftmuth und geduld.
> With meekness, patiently.

Will ich, sein jünger, widerschelten
> Shall I, his follower, be rebuking

Da er nicht widershalt?
> Whom he did not rebuke?

Mit liebe nicht den haß vergelten,
> And not, in love, forgive the hatred,

Wie er den haß vergalt?
> As he that hate forgave?

Wahr ists, verläumdung dulden müssen,
> True 'tis, to have to endure scorning's

Ist eine schwere pflicht
> A heavy duty hard.

Doch selig, wenn ein gut gewissen
> Yet blessed, if a happy conscience

Zu unsrer ehre spricht! . . .
> Our honor does reward. . . .

Und wird er, mich zu untertretten
> And if [my enemy] oppress me,

Durch güte mehr erhitzt;
> By good will warmed in heart,

Will ich im stillen für ihn bäten,
> In quiet I'll keep praying for him,

Und Gott vertaun; Gott schützt.[19]
> Trusting in God, my guard.

Finally, if any more proof were desired of how central the theme of forgiveness was in the Swiss Anabaptist outlook, one could turn to a song in an 1856 songbook of South German (Swiss) Mennonites:

Nur wo Lieb ist, da ist Wahrheit;
    Only where love is can truth be;
Ohne sie giebt's keine Klarheit,
    Without her there is no clearness,
Finster sind wir ohne sie.
    We're in darkness without her.
Heuchelnd wirst vor Gott du treten,
    Falsely will you come before God
Wenn du nicht bedenkst beim Beten,
    If forgetting, when you're praying,
Daß er dich zum Bruder zieh'.
    That he draws your brother near.

Denke nicht, der Herzensprüfer
    Don't imagine the Heart-prover
Schau von deinem Wort nicht tiefer
    Does not, past your words, see deeper
Auf das Herzens Sinn und Rath.
    To the counsel of your heart.
Hassest du den Feind, so wisse,
    If you hate your foe, then know that
Daß das Reich der Finsternisse
    The authority of Darkness
Deinen Geist gebunden hat.
    Has your inner spirit bound.

Nur die Sünde sollst du hassen,
    Only sin should you be hating,
Aber Sünder mild umfassen;
    But the sinners be embracing;
Sie zu richten, ziemt dem herrn.
    Judging them belongs to God.

Freut's dich, daß sie sind gebunden
> Are you glad their nature binds them,
Spottest du ob ihren Wunden?
> Do you mock to see them suffer?
Komm, und hilf sie heilen gern!
> Come and help them to be healed!

Willst mit göttlichen Gefühlen
> Do you wish, with godly feelings,
Du in leeren Worten spielen,
> To—with empty words but playing—
Und doch Christi Jünger sein?
> Be a follower of Christ?
Geh zu ihm und lerne leben,
> Go to him, and study living,
Lern im Leben das Vergeben,
> Learn in life to be forgiving,
Im Vergeben selig sein![20]
> In forgiving to be saved!

11

Forgiveness in Context

A NEIGHBOR OF THE AMISH at Nickel Mines, when asked how the Amish would react to their terrible loss, replied that while they would grieve, they would have "more submission" than ordinary folks. This qualification applies as well to the Amish ability to forgive. As we have seen, they forgive from a stance of yieldedness. To abstract the forgiveness, as though it was a self-contained psychological skill, from that submissive framework of faith, is not to understand what is happening. First comes belief, then the willingness to accept from God the capacity to forgive.

In speaking of this topic, Amish preachers can be heard using an awkward coinage: *Uffgeveness*—literally, "giving-up-ness." This is simply a Pennsylvania German equivalent for the concept of *Gelassenheit* we have seen named in an Anabaptist song. It points to the yieldedness that is necessary for Amish life and community to survive. Its functioning can be observed in innumerable ways, related to God, parents, *G'may* (church congregation), and even government. Already in Switzerland, in the decades just after their fellowship was formed, a government official recorded that the Amish were noticeably more tractable than the Reistians (the larger body of Bernese Anabaptists under the leadership of Bishop Hans Reist from which the Amish had separated).

The Amish do not demand "rights," even under a government that guarantees them. They do not raise their voices in public denunciation of what worldly people do. Children do not talk back to their parents. Even in such a simple act as walking from the barn into the house where the congregation is gathering for meeting, the men walk deferentially in the order of their age, beginning with the oldest. The Amish have no reluctance to consider other Christian denominations as "higher churches," with the implication that they themselves are content, even desirous of being, among the lowest. The Amish like to tell jokes on themselves, not on others.

Amusingly, after some Orthodox "Old Believers" in Russia viewed a documentary on the Amish on Moscow television, they spoke enthusiastically about it to an American Mennonite who had grown up Amish in Kansas. The Russians insisted that in the Amish they had finally discovered their spiritual counterparts in America. However, to further verify their conclusion, they wished to know whether the Amish made the sign of the cross with two or three fingers.

Submission is a way of dealing with what cannot be dominated by thought. As an Amish minister observed, we don't argue with the sun for coming up. We relate to the change of seasons by accepting them in their sequence, which has nothing to do with our preference. Most Amish don't use the device of Daylight Saving Time. For them submission, as a way of relating to reality, is also a way of knowing.

Two months after Nickel Mines, a member of the most conservative Amish communities reflected, "*Es muss also gehen*" (it had to go that way). He was probably consciously echoing a statement in the Gospel of Matthew (26:54). It was his simple take on the tragedy. Perhaps he meant that "it" had to happen because *whatever* happens, happens because it has been specifically foreordained in God's providence. A naïve Calvinist might agree from a theological perspective, while to a secular person that attitude may simply sound like irresponsible fatalism. In contrast, in the previous summer a "Calvinist" minister of the Swiss Reformed church, visiting Plain people in Lancaster County, gave a different response: "Who are we to say what God 'must' do?"

As the Amishman was saying, "It had to go that way," one sensed he meant more than simply accepting predestination. He was expressing a stance of acceptance of the fact that a certain thing had happened. Therapy-oriented writers might call this "closure." Preemptive closure, one might say. It was a sense that what had happened need not be replayed in a scenario that imagined the reversing or changing of what was now history. What has happened needs to be let go, leaving it in trust with God, while hoping always that an evil thing need not be repeated.

In accepting the mind of Christ, we covenant with him and each other to forget, not the particulars of what has happened, but the possibility of getting condign satisfaction, by our own definition, for our resentment. When we say, "Forgive and forget," it's not that we will try to erase mentally what has happened. What we forget is the imagination of the right to have emotional payback in a trespasser's punishment.

"Father, forgive them, for they know not what they do," is part of what could be termed the Plain people's soteriology. That is, their take on forgiveness is that it is not so much a topic in itself, as part of their belief in what it means to be saved. On this subject, I have been asked over and over by evangelical and fundamentalist Christians whether the Amish know what "salvation" is and whether they are saved. My reply is to ask what the questioner considers to be salvation. Usually the answer has to do with whether an Amish person uses a certain verbal formula. As a matter of fact, the Old Order Amish are not comfortable with language that locates salvation in purely personal terms. Their spiritual sense is much more in tune with Jesus' statement in the house of the converted tax collector Zacchaeus. When Zacchaeus responds to Jesus by saying that he is going to restore all he has gained by cheating, Jesus says, "Today salvation has come to this house."

The subjective sensation of this—what salvation "feels" like—comes with yieldedness, submission, and obedience. It does not have the tone of a claim that, if a person has used the right verbal formula of "accepting Christ as Savior," he knows that he is "saved." Rather, one can confess one's confidence in the just and merciful God known in Christ. This hope is a humble one, because what is hoped for cannot be earned by anything we do. And it can only be called genuine if it produces in the believer a forgiveness like the forgiveness offered by the God. For the Amish this is not a complicated subject, and so forgiveness needn't require a long psychological explanation. It is neither a skill nor a strategy but a commitment and a condition of the heart. It is an act of obedience to the one who told Peter to forgive seventy times seven.

The willingness to forgive is also closely related to trust in God. If I deeply believe that, in spite of anything "man can do to me," my eternal soul is kept by God, then I will not despair ultimately. I cannot be robbed of what is most precious. Again, if my children have been killed, the One who keeps them will receive them, and they are forever safe. And finally, if I believe God is a God of justice, then I do not need to worry that evil will not be dealt with.

Simple and precommitted as Amish forgiveness may seem, however, we should not imagine that it is "easier" for the Amish than for "normal" people. They do have the unusually strong empowerment of communal support, but by nature they have the usual ensemble of emotions to deal with. And there are extra temptations in a life of submission, temptations that can drive a marginally loyal Amish person to deep frustration, as various counselors will testify. (Some counseling organizations of various validity have worked up Amish clienteles to considerable profit.) With them as for other people, it can sometimes be easier to forgive one's enemy than one's annoying brother.

If anything, the Amish cherish their children and the integrity of their community even more passionately than most. Nothing hurts more than to lose them from the bosom of the family. Visitors to one of the grieving mothers at Nickel Mines found her weary and appearing, even when surrounded by sympathetic guests, "most of the time as if in a world of her own." When one of them complimented the burly Amish grandfather for his people's ready forgiveness, a tear glistened as he confessed, "It's hard."

12
The Factor of Trust

THE "UNFAIR" RANDOMNESS OF ACCIDENTS—what the psalmist calls "the arrow that flies by day"—is as keenly sensed in Amish life as anywhere else. A buggy has little chance to survive contact with a hurtling automobile. There is no divine barn insurance against anti-Amish arson. One can pray for safety, but there is no guarantee or Christian exception from life's conditions. What there is is trust in a righteous and loving God.

The Amish believe that nothing that happens is outside God's will. "I'm not down in the dumps," says an old conservative after disappointing events. "The Lord has his way, and we don't understand it."

Overheard remarks are revealing. A mother tells her inquiring son, "I understand that the Lord does let this happen, but I do not know why."

The father adds, "Really the only way to answer this is to toss it in the Lord's lap and say, 'You take care of it; I can't.'"

To which the mother adds, "But you may ask him to please carry us through."

And still another voice: "If we give it to God, he'll take it and make something good out of it."[21]

"The Lord giveth," wrote an Amish committee to the world. "The Lord hath taken. Blessed be the name of the Lord. Thank you."

As for the girls, "Our loss is their gain." Having been taken before reaching the "the age of accountability," they are now in a better life. No attacker could take that from them. It's the survivors who feel the pain, and they can give that over to God. The little brothers and sisters are encouraged to touch the bodies: "She's cold now, but she's in heaven." In contrast, a suburban ex-Mennonite woman protectively yanks her curious little son away from the edge of a grave being filled.

Valuable insight on the topic of trust comes from Miraslov Volf, an astute evangelical writer who tasted the moral chaos of the post-communist breakup of the Balkan peninsula. It is easier, he writes, for a person who devoutly believes in a just God, one who will execute proper "vengeance," to let go of useless resentment. Christians in Serbia should know this. Instead, the various regions of the former Yugoslavia are full of monuments preserving unresolved vengeful feelings both pro-Christian and pro-Muslim.

Volf's view does not deny the terrible injustices done on either side. But he observes that while a victim may very well feel release in believing his oppressor faces divine retribution, the difference for a Christian is that he himself won't take up what he believes is God's role in carrying it out.[22] When humans do seize that divine prerogative, they create hell on earth.

This was a seminal difference in the choice for nonviolence made by Anabaptists at the beginning of their movement—a choice that permanently stamped the peaceful

Editions of the *Martyrs Mirror* from three centuries.

character of their Amish descendants. It is a choice that the Amish do not seek to second-guess. The simple-sounding but not naïve choice, learned from Christ, to trust God rather than impose vengeance on our own terms is the difference between Before and After in human history.

13
The Effect of Community

AWFUL AS IT FELT, the Amish grief was not the "unimaginable emptiness" that afflicted the loner who had killed their children. Theirs was a corporate as well as an individual emotion. Their belief, in essence, is that in Christ God has worked a grand reconciliation by which not the enemy but the enmity is slain. Without sophisticated articulation of an idea, they live in the logic of that cosmic reconciliation that changes the tone of human connectedness.

The forgiveness that the Amishman told a TV interviewer he felt "in my heart" comes out of a covenanted culture. A *corporate* precommitment to live in such an attitude makes forgiveness a possibility beyond the imagination of individualists. If pressed to explain this, a member of the Plain people might simply say, "The way we are raised, you get used to it."

This could be regarded as simply the power of groupthink, which lessens the need for personal moral courage. But that is a double-edged criticism. Many who wield it justify their own lack of obedience to the Sermon on the Mount by claiming that they simply haven't been made by their Creator to be what the Sermon calls for. They aren't wired to be pacifists.

It is only fair, though, to ask whether the Amish outlook on forgiveness in a small-scale context is applicable on a broad, international scale as well. For this the commonly cited scheme of German philosopher Ferdinand Tönnies is helpful. He uses the words *Gemeinschaft* and *Gesellschaft* to name what he considers the two basic kinds of relationship: (1) simple face-to-face communities of home, kinship, and village, or (2) city and political or business corporation.

Obviously, Amish society is a classic surviving example of the first type, *Gemeinschaft*. Its people know each other, eat meals in each others' homes, share the same memories, lingo, and outlook. Family is strong, trust operates by shared covenant, and the individual often places the good of the group above his or her individual freedoms (for example, "Shoot me first"). Not to do so brings shame.

By contrast, notes Tönnies, in *Gesellschaft* (society), individuals and primary groups pool their self-interests when possible in order to gain what they want. Instead of covenants there are contracts (which are readily broken if self-interest so dictates and the civil law does not effectively punish). The connection between parties involved is not trust but "cash." This is how things work in a nation that is made up of a variety of clans, races, and religions.

Simply put, in *Gesellschaft* the various primary groups average their interests. Though this is done for the benefit of the general welfare, the individual is really acting out of his own interest. His or her identity becomes, in comparison to that of a small-group member, less specific—more generic. He or she is bound less by voluntary covenant than by contracts having legal force. Life looks different than it had on the farm or in the village and clan. Ethical questions, including the meaning of forgiveness, are complicated and less interesting.

When persons raised in the *Gemeinschaft*-type mindset of the Pennsylvania Plain people tradition move out into the *Gesellschaft* or larger society, they usually give up—as impractical—the simple applications of the Sermon on the Mount of their heritage. Some who keep on being religious find backing for this in a wholesale accepting of a new interpretive grid in the footnotes of the Scofield Bible, a dispensationalist interpretation that postpones the applicability of the ethic of the Sermon to a future era. Meanwhile, the relatives who have stayed Amish, "having their children to themselves" back a long lane from the road and sending them to a one-room schoolhouse with a twenty-year-old Amish teacher, may be able to continue in terms of the *Gemeinschaft* of their heritage. Sure, say those who have left, but the Amish group is a bounded one that seldom puts its *interior* drama out in public. This gives fuel to evangelical Christians who fault the Amish for having "no witness." Ironically, when their simple Christian ethic is splashed into the mass media, whether by the feature film *Witness* or the sensation of their forgiveness at Nickel Mines, what they believe and represent can reach the attention of millions.

14
The Reasonableness of Forgiveness

A CHRISTIAN ACQUAINTANCE whose wife had an open fling with another man told of how he felt the inner sanctum of his heart had been trashed. Even after she returned and said it had been a mistake, he felt the inevitability of divorce. But while sorting out his options, he was surprised to be given, as a Christian, not only the grace to forgive at a specific moment, but more importantly, the possibility to live in forgiveness.

Of course, it was work. But all told, in the midst of his anguish, he eventually could not think of anything important that he would lose by forgiving—except his "pride." He could choose to see his wife as having temporarily lost her bearings. How human she was, to trade lifelong integrity for momentary flaring desire. How outrageous! How deserving she was of being despised! But at the same time there was another option: the pain-discovered possibility of the unique joy in forgiveness. What, my friend asked himself, would be gained by not accepting this option? And what was his Lord calling him to? What was the satisfaction of wounded pride worth, in the long run? Is forgiveness any more illogical than vengeance?

One source of the energy fueling a refusal to forgive is the inability to forgive oneself, or rather, to accept from God the forgiveness for which one asks. A rising anger, out of proportion to its object, is a telltale sign. In a half-century of church life, this writer has seen multiple cases in which an angry condemnation of fellow church members has been the precursor of the revelation that the accuser has been fighting a losing battle with his or her own temptations. The condemnation one feels is passed on to others.

The wonderful meditative writer Kathleen Norris reaps rich lessons of spirituality in the barren landscape of North Dakota, where she has discovered the fellowship of Benedictine monks. Their founder, Benedict, she reports, laid down the requirement that they pray the Lord's Prayer *a minimum* of three times a day.

And this is not a mere device. "Christians believe," as Norris puts it, "that Christ himself is behind the mystery of whatever unity they maintain, and they find in this a sign of hope." Christ is the source and the logic of forgiveness. His mentality is what makes sense. This is the reasonableness Christians live by.[23]

On a television program in the 1970s I was asked to comment on Amish behavior and values. I said the usual things about the obvious: the buggies, the clothes, the rules, and so on. The interviewer seemed to want more; why do they *really* live as they do? I answered that what we were looking at here was a *religious* people and that the key to who they were was their faith. There was a reasonableness, not just an oddity, in their way of thinking. What lingers in memory was how, when I turned to the dimension of their faith, the interviewer's eyes glazed. He wanted *real* insight.

15
The Conundrum of Shunning

THE AMISH BELIEVE that order brings blessing and promotes love. But why doesn't their impressive willingness to forgive injury rule out their practice of ostracizing members who breach their "order"? Where is the forgiveness in shunning dissidents? Why do erring members have to kneel before the congregation in order to be taken back in? Is this love or punishment?

This is a signature issue, woven into the very beginnings of the Anabaptist tradition as a whole. And the emergence in 1693 of an Amish fellowship out of Swiss Anabaptist circles, which was actually mostly about promoting a firmer discipline, was only one of the earliest of a long sequence of wrestlings with this theme. It is not the most attractive feature of the Anabaptist tradition. Yet were it not for their extra-careful definition of boundaries, there would be no Amish. Requiring hooks and eyes instead of buttons and forbidding mustaches are only specific expressions of the larger issue of an accountable membership. If we simply react to the strictness, we will not get far in understanding Amish mentality. To appreciate its inner logic, we can turn again to the scriptural sources on which Anabaptists like

Conrad Grebel of Zurich had focused even before the first baptisms.

Two passages from the Gospel of Matthew, in chapters 5 and 18, are key here. The fact that both of them have to do not with doctrine but with human relationship is already an insight into Anabaptist concerns. The topic of how humans get along with each other is really at the heart of Anabaptist mentality. In that *social* dimension as well as in *personal* faith, one can talk about being "saved." Luther's great discovery was that even though we can never be good enough to be saved, God saves us. By comparison, the Anabaptists' joy was that humans can be made good—that is, peaceful and reconciled according to the pattern of relationship taught and exemplified in Jesus. Here Luther warned: Don't think unrealistically that you can or will be really like that—loving your enemies, blessing them that curse you, and so forth. Though of course we should be, it's wrong to think we can be that good. That's what God's grace is for.

Not so fast, replied the Anabaptists. What was the Sermon on the Mount given for, if we can't obey it?

"To bring you to despair," answers Luther, "so you will throw yourself on the grace of God. Otherwise, you will deceive yourself. You will be a fanatic." While containing valuable truth, this answer did not satisfy Anabaptists.

The issue became humorously personal for this writer when asked to preach "a Mennonite or Anabaptist sermon" in the chapel service of a Lutheran seminary. I went straight to Matthew 5, and took for a text verse 24, "Leave your gift at the altar, and go." That is, I spoke from the Anabaptist feeling that religion that is only personal, without reconciliation, is not valid. If you are at the altar, says Jesus (for example, worshipping at church), and remember that you aren't reconciled with your brother, leave off the otherwise pious praying and *first* be reconciled. *Then* pray. There is a priority here. It is not just in a changed relationship of my heart to God, but also in the effect on the relation of heart to heart that I will feel the effect of salvation.

I can report that my friendly Lutheran hearers found me to be a bit of a fanatic whose message might frighten people away from, rather than invite them to, the altar of worship. Over the coffee and buns, I was informed that Luther wasn't very high on the book of Matthew. He liked Romans and Galatians. As a loyal Anabaptist I rebutted, "I knew Luther didn't like our favorite book of James, but where will this selectivity stop?"

For Anabaptists, worship must not be separated from human relations. The kingdom of God is *about* relationship, not about abstract doctrine. In connection with this theme, Mennonites have found a key focus in chapter 18 of Matthew. In fact, the simple phrase "Matthew 18" is well-known shorthand among Anabaptists for their concept of church. That chapter contains Jesus' classic instruction on how to deal with breaks in human relations. "If your brother sins against you," talk to him personally, and look for restoration of the relationship. If he won't listen, take one or two other persons to the discussion (to see whether it's just you who has the problem).

If he still won't listen, tell it to the group (the *ecclesia*, or "circle"). Though in translations from the Greek the word *church* is used here for *ecclesia*, when Jesus was speaking it could not yet have referred specifically to an institution.

Still, the principle laid down here would be the "order" of the Christian church when it took form at Pentecost.

What comes next in the procedure Jesus teaches can sound harsh, even cruel. When a person who has not listened to one or two others also rejects the counsel of the *ecclesia*, "Let him be to you," says Jesus, "as a heathen and a tax collector." What did that mean in Jesus' time and place? *Heathen* (literally, a non-city-dweller) means roughly "nonreligious," and "tax collector" was practically synonymous with "cheater."

Before we take this to mean that we are to despise such persons, we should remember that Jesus himself socialized with tax collectors and had friendly relations with non-Jews. So what he means in his statement regarding the person who rejects the counsel of the circle is that he may be told, "We'll be neighbors, and we'll treat you as fairly as anybody else, but we won't call it church." In effect, you are not in the church if you don't listen to it. Just as, if as batter you want to call balls and strikes yourself, it's not baseball.

One result of this concept of membership is that the Amish approach the celebration of the Lord's Supper (communion) with great care. That occasion is not only a eucharist (a meal of thanksgiving); it calls for a review of whether those partaking are in a state of reconciliation with each other. Has the reconciliation worked by the shedding of Christ's blood, which is communally celebrated in the Supper, actually been accepted, or is it taken for granted, even when those taking the bread and cup are not unified in spirit? In order to answer this concern, a precommunion inventory of relations "dare never be omitted," as a nineteenth-century Mennonite minister put it. Only this kind of communion can celebrate "the right fellowship with each other with bread and wine in memory of the great love and blessing that Christ has shown to us" (*die rechte Gemeinschaft wider einander mit Brot und Wein*).[24]

That careful concern for harmony within the body is considered by the Amish to be a form of love. Determining that someone is not in harmony with the order of the church is "not a hate thing," a former Amishman tells me. "It's about helping you back in."

This is the tone of the thirteenth stanza from the Hans Buchel song quoted above from the *Ausbund* about how discipline of an erring member is to be approached:

Richt keinen Menschen unverhört,
 Judge no one whom you have not heard;
Man redt oft viel, ein Sach verkehrt,
 Much talk often confuses things,
Viel besser wär geschweigen.
 Silence would be much better.
Daraus erwächsen falsch Gerücht,
 From such develop false reports,
Rott, Secten, wir man täglich sicht,
 Divisions, as one daily sees,
Geistlich Aufruhr und Kriegen.
 Mental uproar and warrings.
Brauch rechte Maß in allem Ding,
 Always discern with care, and if
Sicht du dein Bruder irren,
 You see your brother straying
Mach es nicht groß, auch nicht zu ring,
 Don't blow it up, nor make it small;
Gang selbst hin, thu ihn führen
 Go to him, try to guide him
Für Gottes Kind ohn Argelist,
 With openness, as God's own child;

> *Sein Handel solt erklären,*
> You'll see in his behavior
> *Wann er entgegen ist.*[25]
> If he's opposed to you.

It is important to realize that the Amish do not shun the fellowship of persons who are not members of their covenanted church. Amish homes are generally hospitable to non-Amish neighbors and even strangers. What shunning is about is how to relate to someone who "on bended knee" has vowed in the presence of the covenanted circle to obey Christ and the church and then leaves that particular covenant.

In Matthew 18 Jesus further instructed his followers to make moral decisions that would both "bind" and "release" members of the circle. Behind this function would be the authority of heaven. Jesus did not say the circle would never make a poor call; what he did say was that they had the heavenly mandate to *make* calls. A person who "joins the church" accepts its authority to make moral calls and, with it, the responsibility to "give and receive counsel," that is, participate in its discerning. A natural response is to say, "But how can we fallible humans take up such a responsibility?" Jesus' comment is, "Where two or three of you are together in my name, I am with you."

In one sense, of course, only God can forgive sins—and we must make no pretensions that we are God. If God in Christ would forgive on the cross, we can imitate that forgiveness. When a person turns back and accepts the church's authority to correct him, he is to be forgiven and his disobedience forgotten. The practice of forgiveness is a required part of the right fellowship.

Darnach, laß Gott den Richter seyn,
> Thereafter let God be the Judge,

Gedenk ihm nach, o Bruder mein,
> Take thought for him, O brother mine,

Thu Gott nicht widerstreben,
> With God do not be striving.

Betrüb kein Menschen nimmermehr,
> Give grief to no one evermore,

Den ledig zählt dein Gott und Herr.[26]
> Whom God your Lord counts as released.

That this stress on an accountable membership is as much Mennonite as Amish is made clear in a song by a Mennonite bishop in Lancaster County in 1818. "Pequea" Christian Herr, a successful farmer and county commissioner from West Lampeter Township, had neglected spiritual duties until nearing forty. But when he yielded to the call of Christ and his church, he quickly became its most eloquent spokesman, expressing his repentance and thanks in poems that were almost immediately included in the next edition of the *Unpartheyisches Gesang-Buch*, from which the Amish sing today. One of Herr's best songs deals with the favorite Anabaptist passage of Matthew 18. It is a lyric affirmation of the spiritual accountability Herr himself had declined for two decades. While it is milder than the song last quoted, it makes the very same case: it's necessary to have church discipline. And the conclusion—on how to treat an offending brother—is just as loving:

Wenn Lieb' nicht bricht das herze,
> If love his heart won't soften,

So ist's bedauernswerth,
> It is regrettable;

Dann stelle ihn mit Schmerze
　　　　Then, but with pain, dismiss him
Hinaus zur Zöllner-Heerd,
　　　　Out to the publicans,
Bis dass sein Herze bricht,
　　　　Until his heart may break,
Und sieht die Sünd' im Licht;
　　　　And clearly see the sin;
Dann wird's ihn sicher reuen,
　　　　Then he will surely rue it,
Weil er gehorchet nicht.
　　　　That he has disobeyed.

Dann thut ihn wider lösen,
　　　　And then you must release him
Als Bruder zur Gemein,
　　　　As brother in the church,
Weil er gelöst von Sünden,
　　　　Since he's released from sinning,
Durch Gottes Gnad' allein;
　　　　Through grace of God alone.
Und rück's ihm Niemand auf,
　　　　And do not keep account
Weil er in seinem Lauf
　　　　That he, in his career,
Ein'n Fehltritt hat begangen,
　　　　An error has committed,
Denn du kannst fallen auch.[27]
　　　　For you can fall as well.

　　The Amish could sing such forgiving words with appreciation because at bottom they think of discipline as all about love—love for both the individual and the *gemeinde* (body). Their best leaders recognize that their exceptionally strict way of "doing church" has to avoid two extremes: an inflexible clinging to an order for its own sake on the one hand and on the other hand a relaxing of order for the sake of a freer spirituality. Historical examples show that if they take the latter option, two generations later they are likely to have little left of their particular Anabaptist heritage. ("Spiritual" people think that would be acceptable.) If on the other hand they err in emphasizing form too much, at least, after two generations, they will have that form to work with—the form from which a witness could still bloom brightly in October of 2006.

16
Counsel from Spiritual Cousins

AMONG THE FLOOD of sympathetic messages coming to the Amish of Nickel Mines was one from a Hutterite community in Alberta. Its words showed the closeness of Anabaptist parallel. Directed to "all the families of the senseless slaughter of innocent Children," the letter cut right to the core: "One cannot begin to imagine the feelings and pain that you are enduring. However, you are in our mind, so please accept our Prayers and Sympathy in our absence."

With typical Hutterite directness, the writer acknowledged times when persons may well ask, "Where are You, God? . . . Where was God when we needed Him?" The answer given is the typical Anabaptist close identification with Christ: "The same place He was when Jesus was on the cross. He was right there, as He always is with all His children. . . . Take courage. You are not alone. . . . 'Blessed are those that mourn for I will comfort them.'"

Of course, the Hutterite writer continued, even for those who trust God, "Death has never been easy to accept. We only find comfort in knowing that our loved ones are in a much happier place. Also, knowing that in Christ there are no goodbyes, and that it is in death that we have eter-

Hutterite young people in Alberta, Canada.

nal life, makes things a bit easier." Such words might just as well have come from an Amish writer.

Similarly parallel had been Hutterite and Amish feelings in the previous year or two on the related topic of reconciliation. This theme had been talked up among European descendants of regimes that had persecuted the ancestors of both Anabaptist groups. Now Mennonites, Amish, and Hutterites were all finding themselves invited by persons in Switzerland and Austria to accept an acknowledgment by Europeans of the cruel actions of earlier centuries.

Such an "admission," coming "after so many years," struck the Hutterite letter-writer as "astounding" and hardly looked for, but still deserving of a hearing. When forgiveness is asked for, Christians dare not ignore the request. In a case like that, the writer admonished his fellow American

Anabaptists, "We ought to heed the words of Colossians 3:13: 'Be . . . ready to forgive; never hold grudges. Remember, the Lord forgave you, so you must forgive others.' 'Love your neighbor as yourself.'"

But even that—Christ's golden rule of "what you would like men to do to you, do to them first"—does not cover the whole picture. There is a higher standard in the Sermon on the Mount. "Whoever wants to strive for perfection is obliged . . . to love all who hate and despise him as well."

Anyone accustomed to the manner of the Old Order Amish finds them cautious in responding to spiritual initiatives directed at their covenanted life from non-Amish sources. Often, when they have been admonished to take up this or that attitude, they have felt that those doing the admonishing are also inviting them to change their church loyalties. Were there no reluctance to follow the suggestions of would-be reformers, there would soon be no Amish to reform. And even with their protective stiffness acknowledged, it would be wrong to think that they would not be sympathetic to persons asking for forgiveness.

What they are likely to say, as the Hutterite observer put it, is that "Our forefathers and we have prayed a long time ago already and often with Jesus Christ, 'Father, forgive them; for they know not what they do' (Luke 23:34), and [remembered in] our daily prayers, 'For if ye forgive men their trespasses, your heavenly Father will also forgive you: But if ye forgive not men their trespasses, neither will your Father forgive your trespasses' (Matthew 6:14-15); and 'Let all bitterness, and wrath, and anger, and clamor, and evil speaking, be put away from you, with all malice: And be ye kind one to another, tenderhearted, forgiving one another, even as God for Christ's sake hath forgiven you' (Ephesians 4:31-32)."

"Certain conflicts," concludes the Hutterite writer, "can only be resolved with forgiveness." And he takes pains to spell out a logic familiar to the Anabaptist mentality. "Love flows from faith; for where there is no faith there cannot be love, and where there is no love there cannot be faith. The two are so entwined that one cannot be pleasing to God without the other. Perhaps we can relate to Jesus when he bows his knees before his disciples and washes their feet. You can be sure Jesus knows the future of these feet he was washing. These twenty-four feet will not spend the next day following their master, defending his cause. These feet will dash for cover at the flash of a Roman sword. Yet Jesus forgives their sin before they even commit it. He offers mercy before they even seek it.

"Remember, the secret of being a *nachfolger Jesus Christus* [disciple of Jesus Christ] is to shift our glance away from the one who hurts us and set our eyes on the one who has saved us.

"Jesus washes our feet for two reasons. The first is to give us mercy; the second is to give us a message, and that message is simply this: Jesus offers grace; we are to offer grace. 'But,' we Anabaptists are saying, 'we've done nothing wrong, we're not the one who chopped off the heads, burned them at the stake. We're not the guilty party here.' Perhaps we aren't. But neither was Jesus. Of all the men in that room, only one was worthy of having his feet washed. And he was the one who washed the feet. The one worthy of being served, served others."

Finally, "Forgiving is a serious business because it is

basically for our own spiritual, emotional and physical benefit. We may or may not establish a new relationship with the person who injured us. That is not the heart of forgiveness. When we forgive, we finally stop hurting ourselves, hand the whole matter over to God, and believe what he says: 'Vengeance is mine. I will repay, says the Lord.'—P. M. Wipf, Viking, Alberta."

17
The Universality of Forgiveness

OBSERVING THE MEDIA FASCINATION with the forgiveness at Nickel Mines brought mixed feelings to persons who had been promoting and teaching this theme for years (for example, the Forgiveness Project of London, England, with many incredible stories on its Web site). Forgiveness is not the property of the Amish, as they themselves would strenuously insist. It is a universally known phenomenon, promoted by persons from Hiroshima to Johannesburg, from Belfast to Bangladesh. Its normalcy has been recognized and practiced here and there in many cultures.

There are of course distinct cultural flavors. A Muslim friend reminds me of an issue he faces when dealing with traditional Arab personality. One must always remember, he emphasizes, how intense the sense of personal and familial "honor" is in Arab tradition, to the point that even to my friend it can appear "pathological." At the same time, there are innumerable examples of forgiveness among Muslims (and many other groups) who have been wronged. Just as there is a propensity in radically right-wing "Christian" circles for violent solutions, so there are in some Muslim societies individuals who feel they may or even must kill in order to preserve the family's honor.

Here Christ sets down a fundamental difference, teaching his followers to leave the unacceptable, and the carrying out of "vengeance," up to God, not to their vain wish that things would have happened otherwise.

A thoughtful Muslim comment on the witness of the Nickel Mines Amish appeared on a Web site entitled "Islam in Alaska," under the heading, "Submission To The Will Of Our Creator as described from the thoughts of others." Among the "thoughts" cited were some from Mother Teresa, Albert Einstein, Rabbi Manis Friedman, Pope John Paul II, R. Buckminster Fuller, and ancient Chinese sage Mencius. Then followed an unusual entry entitled "The Amish '3-Rs'":

> I once lived across the road from the Amish in remote southern Indiana farm country. One day, over pie and coffee, after returning their strayed milk cow, we got to discussing why the Amish don't educate their children past the eighth grade. "You folks think we neglect our youth because we don't pursue a higher education for them past the eighth grade. But we feel that this is our most crucial time period for teaching what we feel is an even higher education than your 'higher' education. We admit your higher education is the better advantage for this world, but we feel to educate the heart is more important than educating the head. Yes the head determines one's advantages in this world, but in the higher world, the next world, the eternal world it is the heart that determines one's advantages. So you have your 3-R's and those are good. But we Amish have our 3-Rs also: Responsibility, Reliability and Respect. These are the 3-Rs that build and maintain the kingdom of heaven, on earth or in heaven, without which either kindness or mercy cannot but only briefly last. We plant these as seeds when our kids are tiny and then when they reach those crucial young adult years

just before baptism and marriage, we begin an intensive cultivation process of those 3-R seedlings so they will put down deep sturdy roots. This makes both this life AND the next so much easier, let alone marriage."

The posting of this memory illustrates how Muslims and Christians can appreciate some of each other's central values. Of course one should not imagine that there are no important differences. A central Christian belief that Muslims do not accept is that the Messiah has died for the world's sins. They cannot imagine that a sovereign God could suffer or that the Messiah could be crucified if he was a true prophet. The Qur'an, in fact, states that the Messiah was not really killed; it was just made to look as though he was. To believe this would rule out a central element of what the Amish believe: that their own suffering is to reflect and participate in that of Christ. In the Muslim view, there is no *kenosis*—the pouring out of the self of God or of those who accept this pouring out in themselves. It is more respectful to acknowledge than to ignore such a difference.

There is certainly ground to share. The perhaps atypical Webmaster of "Islam in Alaska" (whose name is given as shakur-abdel-Haleem) claims "both the Amish and the Hutterites" as his brothers and sisters. He views them as "today's longest continuously burning lights of G-d."

"Until we Muslims," he concludes, "succeed in winning our just begun reformation, then it IS these people who demonstrate the only example today on earth of a civilization ruled by Submission, the meaning of the word Islam. Their civilization is going on five hundred years old now—nonstop. May the peace and blessings of Allah be with them all."

18
Musings: Anger, Anguish, and Irony

IN TALKS ON THE THEME of forgiveness as raised by the events at Nickel Mines, this writer has been repeatedly struck by the puzzlement on the faces of persons asking, "How is that type of ready forgiveness humanly possible?" The sense of mystique seems genuine. Is this attitude really something for everybody, or just a minority? It would be doubly sad if these reflections would simply drive a reader to despair.

Glib claims of forgiveness are certainly less to be respected than honest confessions of anger. For a page or two, then, before demanding that all anger be silenced, let us give it some oxygen.

Young Conrad Grebel himself, the first Anabaptist baptizer, grew faint with anger at what he considered the corruption of the church-state network in his native Zurich.

"I am so full of speech," he wrote to a friend, echoing a passage in the book of Job, "that the breath strains my belly, which is swelled as tight as a barrel of new wine without a vent." Again, "You don't believe how it irritates me to watch the educated pastors, the leaders themselves, fouling the water which they lead their flocks to drink."

Or, reading in the *Martyrs Mirror* of a later century, we find the earnest Dutch author interjecting, "Oh dreadful injustice!" as he records the experience of persecuted Swiss Anabaptists. Such outrage was the healthy response to the reports of outrageous oppression.

A Jewish editorialist responded to the Nickel Mines story of forgiveness by asking whether we would really want to live in a world where forgiveness is always instantly given. Anger can be part of the legitimate feeling that some things are intolerable. Thus not all anger is wrong—certainly not the righteous indignation of a genuine prophet. At one point, we read, Jesus "looked around at them with anger" (Mark 3:5). The Amish would understand this.

What is sin is not anger per se, but *wrathfulness as temperament*, and the resultant disrespect for the image of God that is in every person. Plain people honor the scriptural admonition, "Give place unto wrath" (Romans 12:19 KJV), and often quote, "Be ye angry and sin not; let not the sun go down upon your wrath" (Ephesians 4:26 KJV). That is, do not let anger control you. "Let nothing be done through strife" (Philippians 2:3 KJV). "The wrath of man worketh not the righteousness of God" (James 1:20 KJV). This is certainly a reiterated motif in the New Testament. Even the progressive Mennonites and Brethren found it inspiring, in a new hymnal of 1992, to resurrect an old spiritual song on the topic:

> And is the gospel peace and love!
> Such let our conversation be;
> The serpent blended with the dove,
> Wisdom and meek humility.

Whene'er the angry passions rise,
And tempt our thoughts and tongues to strife,
To Jesus let us lift our eyes,
Bright pattern of the Christian life.

Oh, how benevolent and kind,
How mild! How ready to forgive!
Be this the pattern of our mind,
And these the rules by which we live.[28]

A beautiful exhortation. But even given such a mandate, what forgiveness can we feel for a Ceausescu, a Hitler, a Mengele, an Idi Amin, a Pol Pot, a Stalin, or a Saddam Hussein and sons? How can we honestly react with anything but anger to treachery, torture, the rupture of troth that steals a trusted future, or the confiscation of patrimony, whether Naboth's vineyard or the prairies of America's Original People? How forgive the unfaithful spouse or someone who has financially dealt me out of my homestead? Someone who destroys evidence? Who burns other persons' heirlooms? Who shoots an innocent person, leaving him paralyzed for life? Who drives drunk and then blames the driver who didn't get out of her way?

What about the ghastly footage of people leaping into trenches to be shot by the SS in World War II? The men at Srebrenica, bused away as though being taken to work? The unbearable sense of doom in the hysterical chatter of the crowds being herded by Serbian henchmen, who will go back to their own hearths after this day's obscene job is done? The wicked countenance of General Mladic reassuring anxious children and wives, with a smile of anticipation for the massacre of their husbands, fathers, and sons?

Forgiveness, anybody?

There is certainly a legitimacy of anger, a God-given sense of wanting justice done. One feels an unbidden reflex of satisfaction at Auschwitz when a guide, having just led viewers past the shoes and hair of the mass-gassed victims, points out the gallows erected for the camp's commandant, just outside the door of his pleasant house.

Is there a more tender need than a mother's to feel that the sacrifice of her son was for an honorable cause? Or a bitterer rage if she feels that his sacrifice was a waste?

Who suffers more abominably and interminably than a victim of rape, whether by crazed soldier, a fellow prisoner, or a patriarchal guardian of her own hearth? What agony can match the helpless sensation of abuse by persons who should be the very guarantors of trust? What cruelty it is to say simply, "Get over it." Being asked to forgive a person stronger than me, who keeps on hurting me, can simply add bewilderment to pain. Abusers themselves, when exposed, are all for forgiveness, as even Saddam Hussein, facing execution, suddenly called for forgiveness and a handshake all around—such as he himself had not given.

Is there a more exquisite sauce on the meal of the cheated than the pious hypocrisy of the cheater? Or a bitterer irony than in the words of the hymnist who foisted life-cursing opium on a benighted Chinese people, then wrote, "Bane and blessing, pain and pleasure / By the cross are sanctified"?

Still, there is a sad irony in the effect of strident voices limiting abused persons to the enjoyment of anger in their mature decades, when a deeper release is also possible. It's certainly hard work to defeat entrenched patriarchalism, which should be exposed for what it is. But bitterness is little more attractive an option than the cruelty under which one has suffered. The "right" to bitterness in itself brings little healing.

How can we bear to read, "Happy shall he be that taketh thy little ones and dasheth them against the stones" (Psalm 137:9 KJV)? On the one hand, what language is more cathartic than the moans of King David's repentance? On the other, is there a more dangerous prayer than his "Do not I hate them that hate thee?" Yes indeed, "I hate them with perfect hatred" (Psalm 139:21-22 KJV). How different in spirit is this great king's dying instruction not to let his opponents Joab and Shimei die in peace from the spite of Saddam Hussein on the scaffold, cursing "the traitors, the Americans and the Persians"?

Irony upon irony.

In it all, Christians look beyond David the King to one born in the City of David. They hear his voice saying, "Love your enemies," and praying, "Father forgive them." They long for God to rectify the world's pain. They hear the cry of the souls under the altar in the book of Revelation: "How long, O Lord, holy and true, dost thou not judge and avenge our blood on them that dwell on the earth?" (6:10 KJV). But they expect that victory will come by a conquering—a slain—Lamb. Waiting, they have the option of exercising "the patience of the saints." That would be the Amish way.

19
Little Stories

POSTMODERN PEOPLE, according to philosopher Jean-Francois Lyotard, are not convinced of the truth of the "grand narratives" that justify our ethnic, patriotic, or cultural points of view. Under critical examination, these "metanarratives" turn out to be projections, as much propaganda as they are story. There is less reason to be suspicious of the little stories (*petits récits*) of local reference whose modest meanings are clear at least where they sprang up. Without claiming universal applicability, they carry power simply in what they are. Any "little story" carries some meaning for an attentive listener. It is in telling and hearing little stories that a community shapes young minds.

The first images this writer learned of in school were part of the national metanarrative. Above the blackboard were the flag and portraits of George Washington and Abraham Lincoln. We were taught the names of the Nina, the Pinta, and the Santa Maria. Indians living in the "wilderness" helped to celebrate the first Thanksgiving. The blood of brave patriots who had defended liberty was recalled in crimson on the flag. A little cousin, tossing her

In the 1970s the bold simplicity of traditional Amish quilts caught the attention of the art world.

pretty head, was taught to sing to me, "Soldier boy, where are you going, waving so proudly the red, white, and blue?" And I, not knowing what a soldier was, sang back, "I'm going to my country where duty is calling." Seven decades later, though the metanarrative has given way to other truth, the remembered melody can bring back the old chills at the applause of the eighth-graders.

We never heard anything *specific* about the Native people our Swiss-German settlers had replaced, nor, for that matter, anything more than the vaguest clichés about our own people buying wooded tracts north of Philadelphia. We heard only the grand narrative of "America." It would have felt quite different to have been presented with the actual language imposed in 1684 on the friendly Lenape chief or sachem who "sold" to William Penn the land we were living on: "Upon my own Desire and free offer I Maughoughsin in consideration of Two Match coats, four pair Stockings, and four bottles of sider, do hereby grant and make over all my land upon the Perkiomen, to William Penn . . . forever, with which I own myself satisfied, and promise never to molest any Christians . . . that shall seat thereon by his orders." Of course, had we read those words then, we would hardly have realized that these were the words not of the sachem, but of the white bargainers who presented them on the sheepskin they asked him to endorse.

By the time sixteen "deeds" like this had been signed, and there was no more land to be gotten from the Lenapes, they had another titular head, named Sassoonan. As his region of birth had filled with Europeans, he had moved with most of his people one hundred miles to the northwest and saw his boyhood home only on visits. In 1728 he expressed concern that his children would wonder why all their homeland had been deeded away and why some of it, for which no gifts had been given the Indians, was simply being settled by newcomers. But after these complaints, he had touchingly conciliatory words. "He hopes," noted a secretary, that the "good Times" the Indians have had

> ever since the Christians settled here . . . will still continue so long as the Sun & the Light shall Endure, & desires there may be no Coldness between us, so as to hurt them, or any of their or our Children. . . . What he now says comes from his heart, & he speaks honestly & sincerely,

for they are not as Words that come from the Mouth & are no more thought of. . . . He hopes all the differences . . . will be buried deep & covered from the Sight, that when our & their Children in after times, observe the great Friendship that has been between us, it may rejoice & gladden their Hearts. And he hopes that all Differences are buried, & that the Earth round about is made so smooth & Even that their Children may afterwards say; This is the Place where our Fathers & our Brethren . . . Ended & composed all their Differences, so that now there remains no ffootsteps of them.[29]

Such eloquently forgiving words were not shown to us who had made Sassonan's land our own for eight generations. In contrast, our most progressive Mennonite leader had written in 1849 that one reason our busy people had little learning was that the "wild people had persecuted, plundered and killed" the immigrants with "their tomahawks and scalping knives."[30] It was pure metanarrative, and in our local case, totally baseless.

Sometimes our country's grand narrative is simply referred to as "the American Dream." Since its tone of individual self-aggrandizement was not the gospel taught by our humble heritage, our people occasionally told the story of Mennonite Bishop Jacob Kulp, our conference moderator until his death in 1875. Prospering on his farm (now replaced by suburban housing tracts), he became known for lending money. His records of the loans were written on the interior wall of a small washhouse. At least once, after it had become time to whitewash the walls, the person assigned the task told the bishop that this would obliterate the records of what was owed. Instead of changing his mind, the bishop gave directions to go ahead. It was time to whitewash, and God knew who still owed and how much.

There was the man in Ontario who got on the nerves of the joint owners of a creamery that employed him. Skilled as he was, they found his personality so annoying that they decided he must be fired. But one of the owners, Gilbert Bergey, was concerned for the man's family. Would the others allow him one more chance to talk to the man? Permission was given, and Bergey communicated so effectively that things ran more smoothly. In fact, this bit of forgiveness was a success story, the employee remaining with the position for the rest of his life.

A forgiving gesture by Henry Rosenberger, a Mennonite farmer in Bucks County, Pennsylvania, became a part of local memory. A leading officer in a bank at Chalfont, he consented to sign a note on behalf of a borrower from the bank. On the day the note came due, the borrower appeared at the bank to ask that it be renewed. He had been to Rosenberger's home, he said, only to find him away. But he surely would have signed, said the borrower, had he been there. That was his reputation. On the basis of this account, the officer of the bank who happened to be there refrained from imposing the penalty for not meeting the obligation, only to find that the borrower was declaring bankruptcy, and the money was lost. When Rosenberger next appeared at the bank, he was told that he was lucky he had not been home to sign, because now he was not responsible for the loss. "He used your name," said the officer. Rosenberger replied, "Let me see the note." Then, taking a pen, he signed his name. This was *Gemeinschaft* exercised in a setting of *Gesellschaft*, with the individual forgiving the debt in the name of the community.

In fourth grade I sat with a friend during an arithmetic drill. The teacher, then in her first year, directed us to sit in perfect stillness until she gave the signal to start our chant. Alas, my mischievous buddy and I felt the silent tension mounting until we burst out together in disruptive giggling. As we then cringed, we were gratefully shocked to hear the teacher say, "That's all right, boys, I know this can make you nervous." The tone of her response was so different from the reprimand we awaited that it was a little, never-to-be forgotten epiphany: forgiveness is an option.

My grandfather, a man of genial kindness, had a competitor in the Philadelphia market hall where they both had "stands." The man, also from our community, had taken offense at some deal or other. From then on he refused to speak to my grandfather, and crossed the street rather than walk by him. Instead of reacting in kind, my grandfather would always wave and say hello. For a long time there was no change. Then the report came that the offended man had fallen seriously ill and was calling for my grandfather. At bedside the man asked to be forgiven for his attitude, and from then on the two market men—one Mennonite and one not—remained friends. My grandfather's taking the time to tell me this little story carefully showed me he hoped I could learn its lesson.

Cheyenne Peace Chief and Mennonite minister Lawrence Hart of Oklahoma is a powerful storyteller. The violence experienced by his ancestors at the hands of American soldiers lives in his memorable narration of the attack in 1868 by General George Armstrong Custer on a sleeping Cheyenne village on the Washita River. These were Hart's ancestors, and the story is bitterly ironic, in that it is about a chief, Black Kettle, who was trying to keep peace, not attack, before he was killed in ambush.

The story comes full circle as it recounts a 1968 centennial reenactment of the attack. Having cautiously accepted participation in the occasion, Hart and his Cheyenne relatives were suddenly shocked and angered to find that, unknown to the Cheyennes, grandsons of the attacking Seventh Cavalry had been invited to take part. For them the celebration was of a "battle," whereas the Cheyennes were remembering an unprovoked slaughter. As the unexpected celebrants in full military regalia descended on the village, shooting blanks and singing their grandfather's attack song, "Gary Owen," the Cheyennes felt a rush of fear and ancestral anger for such insensitivity toward their feelings.

But a redemptive moment arrived later in the observance. Hart was asked by the older peace chiefs to react to the celebrating reenactors with a gesture of forgiveness. Obeying this counterintuitive request, he called up the saber-wielding captain of the Seventh Cavalry grandsons, asked him to turn around. Then he draped a blanket over the armed man's shoulders. It was a gesture that melted observers hearts. The battle-costumed rangers' captain, in tears, promised that the Cheyennes would never again have to listen to "Gary Owen," the dreaded battle song of the original attack. The motif of forgiveness had transformed the celebration of violence.

A very "little" story: In the last few weeks of my father's 101 years a visitor from Lancaster County stopped by his bed. It was Amos Hoover, legendary bibliophile, collector of Plain Mennonite lore, and founder of the Muddy Creek Farm Library. Instantly remembering that he had once visited the library in the Hoover home, my father confessed a fear that he might not have properly reshelved a book he had looked at there. Expecting to hear Amos say it didn't matter, I was struck to hear, instead, "Well, you're forgiven." The effect was strangely, humorously healing. My super-conscientious father hadn't been diminished but embraced.

I have been personally touched by the testimony of forgiveness of two local women. The first was abandoned and divorced in middle age by a man looking for more than he found in their marriage. Then, disappointed in further relationships, he contracted terminal cancer and became helpless. His rejected wife became his nurse, voluntarily caring for him while he lived, as though he were still her husband.

The second woman, active in family and church, was made paraplegic when the vehicle of a drunken driver struck hers. Because of the nature of her injuries, she was placed in a hospital bed that moved from side to side, making it impossible even to read. It gave her, she found, "lots of time to think" about her painful and disappointing lot. "One day," she recalls, "I remember thinking about Stephen. He said, 'Lay not this sin to their charge.'" With that, she decided not to blame the man who had struck her, even though he would never show any interest in apologizing. What Stephen's attackers had done, she mused, was "intentional," whereas the man who had hurt her had not gone out in the morning to attack her. "That made a big difference" in her thinking. Further, she asked herself, as a result of the accident, "Whose heart was broken? He had a grandmother and a mother." How must they feel about his behavior? "It could have been worse"—as it was worse in some ways for the parents, wife, and children of the man who attacked the

Amish girls than it was for the girls' parents. What if it had been her own son, thought my friend, who had permanently injured someone else? "I told myself, you can't go back. The man who hit me has a problem. I've solved mine."

"You make a choice," concluded my friend. Of course, "It helps that there are people around you who care."

My brother-in-law, Donald R. Jacobs, served as a missionary in East Africa for a quarter-century. He has brought home many powerful stories. One shared in our own family circle, coming out of the bitter Mau Mau uprising in Kenya in 1969, concludes memorably on the theme of forgiveness and evokes the starkly simple tone of the *Martyrs Mirror*. Jacobs recounts the story in his memoirs:

> One of our favorite helpers was Gladys, a Kikuyu woman who lived about five miles northwest of Nairobi on a little Kikuyu farm with chickens, goats, and maybe a cow. Gladys was one of those touched by the radical gospel in what has been called the East African Revival. She was absolutely committed to following Jesus Christ in strict discipleship. Her husband would have none of it. He was an alcoholic and seldom around. Gladys ran the home, and she did that very well.
>
> She was sustained spiritually by the revival fellowship group that she attended in her community and she was also a dedicated Presbyterian. It was not easy for her to raise her family—she was for all intents and purposes, a widow, even though she was legally married. She was very good for us. When we faced any hardship we reminded ourselves of the way Gladys was facing life in spite of all that loomed up before her. She worked in our house, cleaning, etc., a few days a week. We paid her as much as the local environment allowed and we hired her son, Samson, to work in the yard and do odd jobs. He did that with almost no supervision. Gladys became a part of our household.

It was fall of 1969 when she asked us to pray for her and for those in her fellowship who were being harassed by the Kikuyu tribal oathers. Election time was approaching and the Kikuyu tribe wanted to vote as a bloc for their candidate for president. For this purpose they resurrected an ancient ordeal, the oath which was used, in a political form, during the Mau Mau days of the 1940s and early 50s. The potion itself was a mixture of animal blood and intestinal material, if I recall correctly, served in half a gourd. The idea was that as you drank this potion you swore to obey the commands of the tribal ancestors and if you failed to do so you would suffer a curse.

Most of the Kikuyu people, (22 percent of the nation's population) the largest of the thirty or more tribes in Kenya, drank the oath without protest, if not gladly. The saved ones [Christians] balked at it because they could not possibly swear obedience to anyone other than their Jesus. So the oathers were systematically hunting down all the reluctant ones to force them to take the oath.

Gladys came to work several times with the news that this family had been taken away, then another. Then she shocked us with the news that Evangelist Samuel, the leader of her own fellowship group and a person with whom we were acquainted, was taken away during the night—along with his wife and as I recall, five daughters. They refused to take the oath in their home, and so were taken to the traditional oathing place in the forest, where they again refused. For that they were severely beaten, first Samuel, then his wife and then the daughters. Even after that they refused and so were left alone in the cold forest—stripped naked.

When morning dawned the oathers were back, the potion was prepared, with the same result. Refusal, then a sound beating. Samuel protested, "We have already drunk the blood of Jesus and this blood that you have in the gourd will not mix with that blood that we already drank!"

The brothers and sisters, assuming what had happened, hired a pickup to look for them. They found them at the oathing place beaten. Loading them all on the truck they proceeded to the nearest hospital, a government hospital, where, to their dismay, all the workers had been oathed, and so [Samuel and his family] could not be treated. Samuel, a rather thin, frail man was losing blood. They had to drive a distance to the mission hospital where Samuel died of loss of blood. His wife, of a more robust nature, survived but was badly bruised. The daughters recovered.

Gladys invited us to attend the funeral on a little hill near her place where a little corrugated iron church sat. The place was swarming with people. It had been a while since the last martyr's funeral in Kenya. It hit the news, of course, so the press turned out in great numbers. When we arrived the service had begun. We realized that what had happened transformed the ground on which we were standing, so to speak. Singing, praying, preaching, testifying, the service went on and on.

Then a little white Ford sedan came up the hill and out stepped Samuel's wife, wrapped with bandages. With a warm smile on her face she said that before he died her "brother" Samuel, realizing he could not survive, told her that he forgave his killers and asked that God would forgive them too. She then said, "In the name of Jesus, you are forgiven." We were not right up front to hear and see all this, but it is what happened.

As the congregation then carried the coffin to the open grave several yards away, it turned into a sort of celebration. It seemed like all wanted to touch the wooden coffin. After a service of committal we all gathered around and threw dirt into the hole. When the dirt was heaped, we stood for a final reflection when one of the brethren said, "I need to repent of a sin of selfishness. I found myself wishing I would be in there instead of Samuel. I am sorry. May Jesus forgive me." So things go at a martyr's funeral.

Another oathing death followed in about a week in another part of Kikuyuland. There was such an uproar that the government prohibited any more tribal oathing. The elections that followed were entirely peaceful. Those martyrdoms had produced a harvest of peace more or less immediately, unlike many martyrdoms in church history.

A final *petit récit*. Around the time of the attack at Nickel Mines an international group of scholars studying at the University of Pennsylvania visited our congregation, thirty miles north of Philadelphia. They were taken to the nearby Mennonite Heritage Center, with its then current exhibit on the themes of peace, forgiveness, and reconciliation. Statements from Scripture, Menno Simons, Elie Wiesel, Nelson Mandela, the father of a man beheaded in Iraq, a Mennonite nurse, and others were placed in a kind of time-line. One of the South African visitors seemed especially struck by the exhibit. Her husband, she revealed, had been murdered in the troubles of recent decades. This had left her terminally angry, hating the persons who had caused her pain. But something happened to her as she moved across the exhibit, carefully reading statement after statement of forgive-ness and calls for reconciliation. Overwhelmed by the cumu-lative effect, she flatly informed her fellow students, "I'm not the same person as the one who came in here. When I go back to South Africa, my friends will not know me. I have made the decision to forgive."[31]

20
Coda

A S BISHOP DESMOND TUTU OBSERVED, forgiveness is the best form of self-interest. It is also the best revenge.

No monument will be raised at Nickel Mines. But in hearts around the world there is a fresh echo of the words and example of Jesus Christ.

A people synonymous with holding on have shown how to let go.

A "backward" people have pointed the way forward.

Notes

1. Ishmael Beah, interview on National Public Radio, February 21, 2007.

2. Miroslav Volf, *Exclusion and Embrace: A Theological Exploration of Identity, Otherness, and Reconciliation* (Nashville: Abingdon Press, 1996), 121.

3. Oberammergau is a village in south Germany where, every ten years, a Passion play is performed.

4. Pennsylvania State Rep. Gibson C. Armstrong, 100th Legislative District, Letter to the Editor, *Intelligencer Journal* (Lancaster, Pa.), October 9, 2006.

5. Editorial in the *Los Angeles Times*, in "Other Newspaper Editorials about Slayings," *Intelligencer Journal* (Lancaster, Pa.), October 5, 2006.

6. Ann Taylor Fleming, "Essayist Gains Inspiration from the Amish Community's Ability to Forgive," PBS Online *NewsHour*, October 6, 2007.

7. *Unpartheyisches Gesang-Buch Enthaltend Geistreiche Lieder und Psalmen, Zum allgemeinen Gebrauch des Wahren Gottesdienstes*, 43rd printing (Lancaster, Pa.: Verlag von den Amischen Gemeinden in Lancaster County, Pa., 1999), 474.

8. Lori van Ingen, "Forgiveness is a Matter of Faith," *Intelligencer Journal* (Lancaster, Pa.), October 18, 2006, A1.

9. Anonymous, "*Ein Wahrhaftiger Bericht von den Brüdern im Schweitzerland, in dem Zürcher Gebiet, Wegen der Trübsalen, Welche über sie ergangen sind, um das Evangeliums willen. Von dem*

1635sten bis in das 1645ste Jahr," an appendix to *Ausbund das ist: Etliche schöne Christliche Lieder,* "41 Bekannte Auflage" (Lancaster, Pa.: The Amish Book Committee, 1997), 864.

10. Gerald Biesecker Mast, "The Persistence of Anabaptism as a Vision," *Mennonite Quarterly Review* 81 (January 2007), 20.

11. Peter Riedemann, *Rechenschaft: Translation of the 1565 German edition of Confession of our religion, teaching, and faith, by the brothers who are known as the Hutterites* (Scottdale, Pa.: Herald Press, 1999), 110.

12. *Ausbund,* 624.

13. Ibid., 451.

14. Ibid., 254-5.

15. Ibid., 260.

16. Ibid., 261.

17. *Unpartheyisches Gesang-Buch,* Second part, after the initial Psalm section, 3.

18. Ibid., 259.

19. Ibid., 259-60.

20. Mark Jantzen, "Reviving Songs of Peace from the Vistula Delta," in *Sound in the Land,* Maureen Epp and Carol Ann Weaver, eds. (Kitchener, Ont.: Pandora Press, 2005), 55-6.

21. Daniel Burke, "Amish Search for Healing, Forgiveness After 'The Amish 9/11,'" Religion News Service, October 3, 2006.

22. Volf, *Exclusion and Embrace,* 119-25.

23. Kathleen Norris, *Amazing Grace: A Vocabulary of Faith* (New York: Riverhead Books, 1998), 159-60.

24. The words of Mennonite bishop Hinrich Kassel of Gerolsheim, Germany, in 1681, cited in John L. Ruth, *Maintaining the Right Fellowship* (Scottdale, Pa.: Herald Press, 1984), 19.

25. *Ausbund,* 260-61.

26. *Ibid.,* 261.

27. "A Collection of Hymns, Written by Bish. Christian Herr," in John F. Funk, comp., *A Biographical Sketch of Bish. Christian Herr. Also a Collection of Hymns, Written by him in the German Language* (Elkhart, Ind.: Mennonite Publishing Company, 1887), 19.

28. "And is the Gospel Peace and Love," *Hymnal: A Worship*

Book (Elgin, Ill.: Brethren Press, 1992), no. 406, from Anne Steele, *Poems on Subjects Chiefly Devotional*, vol. 1, 1760.

29. *Minutes of the Provincial Council of Pennsylvania*, vol. 3 (Harrisburg, Pa.: State of Pennsylvania, 1840), 338ff.

30. "A Letter of John H. Oberholtzer to Friends in Germany, 1849," in John C. Wenger, *History of the Mennonites of the Franconia Conference* (Telford, Pa.: Franconia Mennonite Historical Society, 1937), 420.

31. Unforgettable words of forgiveness by Cynthia Ngewu, South African mother of a murdered son, can be read in a transcript of the documentary, "Long Night's Journey Into Day," available on the Internet at www.newsreel.org/transcripts/longnight.htm.